Air Support for
Patton's Third Army

ALSO BY JOHN J. SULLIVAN
AND FROM MCFARLAND

*Overlord's Eagles: Operations of
the United States Army Air Forces in
the Invasion of Normandy in World War II* (1997)

AIR SUPPORT FOR PATTON'S THIRD ARMY

by John J. Sullivan

McFarland & Company, Inc., Publishers
Jefferson, North Carolina, and London

LIBRARY OF CONGRESS CATALOGUING-IN-PUBLICATION DATA

Sullivan, John J., 1925–
    Air support for Patton's Third Army / by John J. Sullivan.
    p. cm.
    Includes bibliographical references and index.

    ISBN 0-7864-1465-0 (softcover : 50# alkaline paper) ∞

    1. United States. Army Air Forces. Air Force, 9th — History.
2. United States. Army. Army, 3rd — History. 3. World War,
1939–1945 — Aerial operations, American. 4. World War, 1939–
1945 — Regimental histories— United States. 5. World War, 1939–
1945 — Campaigns— Western Front. 6. Close air support —
History — 20th century. 7. Patton, George S. (George Smith),
1885–1945. I. Title.
D790.S963 2003
940.54'214 — dc21
                                                      2003001399

British Library cataloguing data are available

©2003 John J. Sullivan. All rights reserved

No part of this book may be reproduced or transmitted in any form or by any means, electronic or mechanical, including photocopying or recording, or by any information storage and retrieval system, without permission in writing from the publisher.

Cover photograph: A Douglas A-20 Havoc fighter/bomber *(National Archives and Records Administration).*

Manufactured in the United States of America

McFarland & Company, Inc., Publishers
  Box 611, Jefferson, North Carolina 28640
    www.mcfarlandpub.com

To the memory of
my brothers,
James, Robert and Richard,
and our mother,
Julia Barry Sullivan

Acknowledgments

The author wishes to acknowledge his large debt to the publications of the United States Army and Air Force, especially *Breakout and Pursuit* by Martin Blumenson, *The Lorraine Campaign* by H. M. Cole, and *The Army Air Forces in World War II*, edited by W. F. Craven and J. L. Cate. He is grateful to the staffs of the following archives, and libraries for their unfailing courtesy and assistance:

- Library of Congress Manuscript Division and library
- United States Army Military History Institute and library
- United States Air Force Historical Research Agency and the Air University library
- United States National Archives and Records Administration's Modern Military Records Division, and the Still Pictures Branch
- libraries of the University of Maryland, University of South Florida, and State University of New York at Albany
- public Libraries of Albany, N.Y., and Sarasota, Florida
- United Kingdom Public Record Office
- United Kingdom Imperial War Museum.

Contents

Acknowledgments vi

Tables, Diagrams, Maps ix

Preface 1

Introduction 3

1. Breakthrough into Brittany 17
2. The Ninth Air Force 34
3. Close Air Support 42
4. The Drive to the Loire 51
5. Ninth Air Force Engineers, Liaison Operations, Interdiction and Communications 62
6. XV Corps at Argentan 74
7. The Third Army Crosses the Seine 82
8. The Drive to the Meuse 90
9. The Capture of Brest 96
10. Air Supply for Ground Forces 106
11. British Receive Priority for Supplies 112
12. The Drive to the Moselle 121
13. Air Support for the Third Army's Autumn Operations ... 135

14. The November Offensive 143
15. The Drive to Bastogne 151
16. Evaluations of Air Support for the Third Army 157

    Glossary 163
    Notes 165
    Bibliography 177
    Index 181

Tables, Diagrams, Maps

TABLES
Ninth Air Force Medium and Light Bombers 31
XIX Tactical Air Command, August–September 1944 34
Bomb Loads and Tactical Radii 44
Liaison Aircraft 67
Tank Characteristics 129
Tons of Cargo Unloaded Daily 142

DIAGRAMS
OVERLORD's Commanders 8
Ninth Air Force 12
Third United States Army 17

MAPS
Area of Operations of Allied Armies, August 1944 9
Brittany 19
XV Corps' Objectives, August 9–12, 1944 75
Major Ferries on the Seine River, August 1944 83
Allied Front Lines, August–September 1944 122
Nancy Area 128
Airfields West of the Third Army, September 1944 136
Metz Area 139
Objectives of the Third Army in Its November 1944 Offensive 144
XII Corps' Front, 8 November 1944 145
Ardennes Area 152

Preface

For seven weeks after the start of the Allied Invasion of Normandy in June 1944, Lieut. General George S. Patton's Third U.S. Army remained in reserve. In late July, as the German front began to crumble, Patton received orders to send the Third Army into battle. Its first objective was to clear German forces from Brittany. During the next seven weeks the Third Army fought across France in one of the most successful campaigns in military history.

Many books and dramas have portrayed phases of Patton's colorful life but none paid much attention to a crucial reason for the Third Army's victories—the air support given to it by the U.S. Army Air Forces, especially the Ninth Air Force.

The Ninth Air Force was organized to give close support to American ground forces assigned to Operation OVERLORD. It had much to learn about cooperating with ground troops but its equipment and key personnel had been tested and honed by combat operations during the pre-invasion period. One of its units, the XIX Tactical Air Command, gave the closest possible fighter-bomber support to the Third Army.

My interest in military air and ground operations stems from personal experience. I worked in communications sections of the U.S. Marine Corps fighter and liaison squadrons during World War II. During the Korean War I served with the 2nd U.S. Infantry Division and experienced the impact of air support for ground troops.

The narrative concentrates on tactical air operations in France in 1944 and their impact on the Third Army. It does not give a biography of General Patton, nor a definitive history of the Third Army. It describes the many technical services that must be given to flight crews and airplanes of a tactical air force if it is to function effectively. Airfields are an obvious necessity with their fuel depots, ordnance, vehicles, tools, communications equipment and ground crews. The Ninth Air Force developed techniques for building airfields quickly and moving groups to them without serious interruptions in operations.

One of the themes of the narrative is logistics. The operations of both the Ninth Air Force and the Third Army were curtailed by shortages of supplies, especially gasoline. Examinations of this failure and its consequences occupy a substantial part of the narrative. The Army Air Forces coped with logistics crises by delivering military supplies in its bomber and transport airplanes.

John J. Sullivan
January 2003

Introduction

The Third United States Army's operations in August 1944 were a dramatic and crucial part of Operation OVERLORD — the Allied invasion of northwest Europe. General Dwight D. Eisenhower, the supreme commander of OVERLORD, knew from the outset that air power would be crucial to the success of the endeavor. He stated this theme: "... one of the fundamental factors leading to the decision for undertaking Overlord was the conviction that our overpowering air forces would make feasible an operation which would otherwise be considered extremely hazardous, if not foolhardy."[1]

Three air commanders worked closely with Eisenhower at the Supreme Headquarters Allied Expeditionary Forces [SHAEF]. Two were Royal Air Force [RAF] officers. Air Chief Marshal Arthur Tedder, the Deputy Supreme Commander, directed SHAEF's air operations. Air Chief Marshal Trafford Leigh-Mallory commanded the Allied Expeditionary Air Forces [AEAF] composed of the British 2nd Tactical Air Force, commanded by Air Vice Marshal Arthur Coningham, and the United States Ninth Air force, commanded by Lieutenant General Lewis Brereton. Leigh-Mallory also coordinated efforts of other air forces when they operated in support of OVERLORD.

Lieutenant General Carl A. Spaatz directed U.S. Air Forces supporting OVERLORD. Eisenhower knew Spaatz well. They had been students together at West Point. Spaatz had commanded U.S. air forces in the Italian and African campaigns. The Chief of the U.S. Army Air Forces [AAF], General H. H. Arnold, considered him to be his ablest field commander. Spaatz and Arnold had been pioneer Army aviators. In World War I Spaatz ran a training center in France and flew several combat missions. He shot down a few German aircraft. In his postwar book Eisenhower thanked "the gods of war and the War Department" for giving him Spaatz.[2]

Spaatz had heavy responsibilities beyond SHAEF. He commanded the U.S. Strategic Air Forces [USSTAF] composed of the U.S. 8th Air Force, operating from the UK, commanded by Major General James Doolittle,

Air Marshal Arthur Coningham and Major General Lewis Brereton (courtesy of the Imperial War Museum, Cu12783).

and the U.S. 15th Air Force, based in Italy, commanded by Major General Nathan Twining. USSTAF carried out strategic bombing campaigns in cooperation with RAF Bomber Command under the direction of the Allied Combined Chiefs of Staff [CCS]. RAF Bomber Command was commanded by Air Chief Marshal Arthur Harris.

With Arnold's full support, Spaatz became the chief AAF officer in the European Theater of Operations [ETO].

To prevent squabbles among U.S. air forces for supplies, equipment and personnel, Spaatz assumed control of all administrative and training matters pertaining to the Ninth Air Force. This reduced the authority of Brereton and Leigh-Mallory over the Ninth Air Force. Spaatz later explained to a historian that Brereton was never in any doubt about who commanded the Ninth Air Force. It was not Leigh-Mallory.

Eisenhower learned to respect Tedder during their association in the African and Italian campaigns. Moreover, he counted on Tedder to obtain full cooperation from the RAF. As Deputy Supreme Commander, Tedder advised Eisenhower about ground as well as air matters. Unfortunately, his relations with General Montgomery soon soured. Monty did not take direction readily from anyone, and certainly not from an airman. His relations with SHAEF's staff turned cool then frigid.

Leigh-Mallory's position seemed well-defined on paper, but in fact he was enmeshed in conflict and hostility. He and Spaatz differed frequently about the Ninth Air Force and other issues. SHAEF's staff believed that Tedder should direct OVERLORD's air operations, a job that Leigh-Mallory considered his. Spaatz believed that Leigh-Mallory was incompetent to direct strategic air forces that were assigned to support OVERLORD. He told Eisenhower that he had "no confidence in Leigh-Mallory's ability to handle the job, and that I view with alarm any setup which places the Strategic Air Forces under his control."[3] In this opinion, Spaatz was supported by Arnold, who believed that AEAF was a redundant organization that put a barrier between the supreme commander and his air force commanders.

Leigh-Mallory's personality disrupted relations with his associates. Even one of his colleagues recalled that he was "so typically English, sometimes tactless, and almost pompous in appearance and naive in character without any finesse, that it was difficult for the Americans to assess his ability ...."[4] Most Americans who worked with Leigh-Mallory believed he held a low opinion of Americans generally. This attitude was widespread among British officers.

Eisenhower had been warned that the commander of the RAF Bomber Command, Air Chief Marshal Arthur Harris, would protest about being

Air Marshal Trafford Leigh-Mallory (left) and Major General E.P. Quesada (courtesy of the Imperial War Museum, LL338).

assigned to support OVERLORD. The forecast proved to be accurate. Harris warned the Chief of the Royal Air Forces, Air Marshal Charles Portal, about the futility (in his opinion) of using heavy bombers to attack gun emplacements and beach defenses. Such use would divert "our best weapon from the military function for which it has been equipped and trained to tasks which it cannot effectively carry out."[5] RAF Bomber Command's best employment, according to Harris, was to bomb German cities at night.

Eisenhower remained unmoved by such complaints. He insisted that all available air power should support OVERLORD under his command. Harris became one of his most loyal subordinates.

Compared to OVERLORD's air organization, the chain of command for its ground forces was a model of clarity. General Bernard Montgomery directed the British 21st Army Group, made up of the Second British Army, commanded by Lieutenant General Miles Dempsey, and the First Canadian Army, commanded by Lieutenant General Henry Crerar. During the landings and subsequent seizure of a lodgment area, Montgomery would also direct the U.S. First Army, commanded by Lieutenant General Omar

Generals Haislip, Patton, Cook and Bradley (courtesy of USAMHI).

Bradley. When logistics and operational conditions warranted, Bradley would take command of the U.S. 12th Army Group, composed of the First Army, commanded by Lieutenant General Courtney Hodges, and Third Army, commanded by Lieutenant General George S. Patton, Jr.

General Patton was born in California in 1885 and spent most of his youth on a ranch near San Gabriel owned by his well-to-do family. His grandmother had left Virginia after the Civil War, in which many of her relatives, including her husband, served in the Confederate forces. Patton decided to pursue a military career and entered the Virginia Military Institute. From there he transferred to the United States Military Academy at West Point. After graduation, Patton served with General Pershing in the Mexican campaign. In France during World War I, Patton commanded a tank battalion. He commanded American forces in the landings in North Africa in 1942 and Seventh Army in the Sicily campaign. Patton narrowly survived several crises caused by his emotional and outspoken nature. After he slapped a wounded soldier in Sicily, many politicians and newspapers demanded his dismissal.[6]

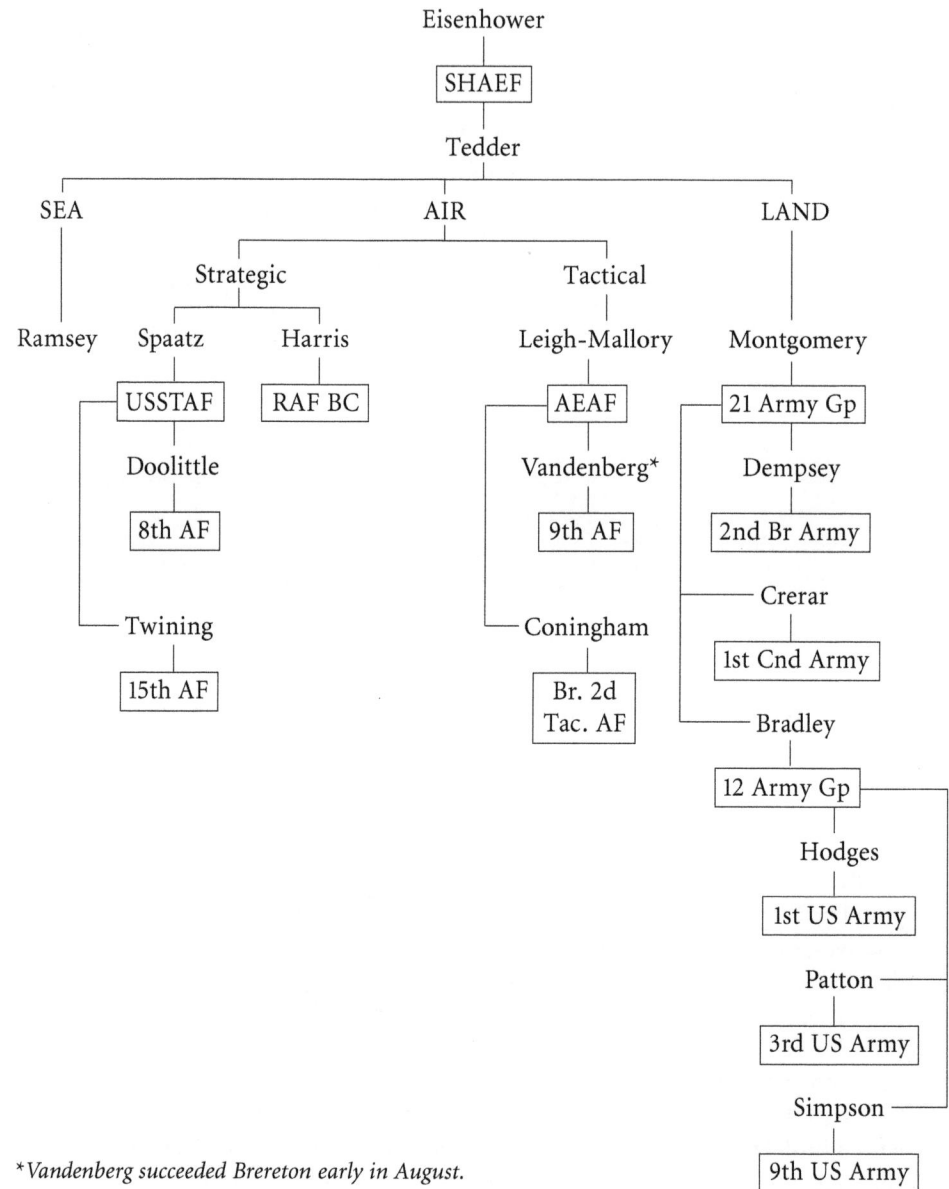

Diagram 1. OVERLORD's Commanders, August 1944.

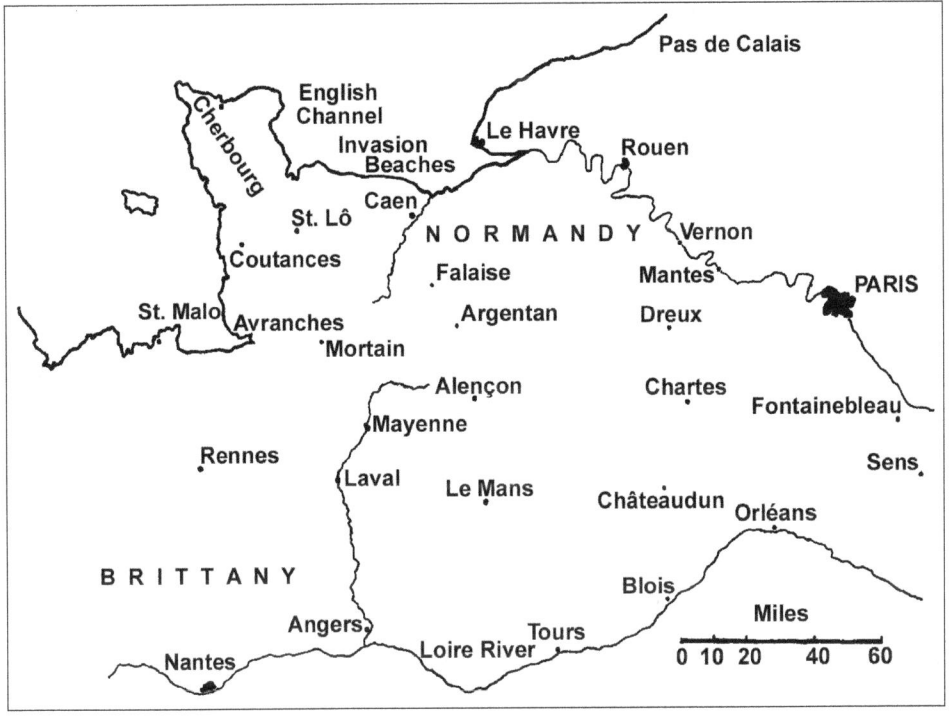

Map 1. Area of Operations of Allied Armies, August 1944.

Although Diagram 1 may be useful as a lineup of Eisenhower's team, it does not show that Spaatz controlled the Ninth Air Force's administration. Nor does it show that the 15th Air Force was a part of the Mediterranean Allied Air Forces. Montgomery's direction of American forces would end when the lodgment area was secured. At that time Eisenhower would assume direction of all Allied ground operations.

Allied armies landed in Normandy on June 6, 1944. During the next six weeks they pushed south slowly as their strength steadily increased. For General Montgomery's 21st Army Group, progress was indeed slow. Repeated attempts to take Caen, a D-Day objective, failed, with heavy losses. Tough German panzer divisions slowed British progress to a crawl.

On the right of 21st Army Group, General Bradley's First Army battled in difficult bocage country, with heavy losses and small gains. The bocage was crisscrossed with thousands of hedgerows which formed enclosed pastures. Hedgerows were walls of earth planted with bushes and trees with tough, twisted roots. German troops skillfully transformed the enclosures into bastions. In this terrain, which was also spotted with swamps and marshes, tanks could not operate effectively. The narrow beachhead did not permit the Allied air forces to set up all the airfields they needed.

On June 27, VII Corps, commanded by Major General J. Lawton Collins, captured Cherbourg, a major port that Allied forces needed badly. For months after D-Day most Allied supplies came through Cherbourg or over the beaches, an inefficient method which choked Allied supply lines.

In June and July, as the First Army pushed slowly southward, Ninth Air Force fighter-bomber units sharpened their ground support procedures. These needed much improvement. During peacetime the Army Air Corps had neglected close air support. It preferred to spend its scarce funds on strategic air war equipment and personnel. Even during the first years of the war Arnold found it difficult to energize the AAF's ground attack program. In December 1942 he sent a sharp reminder to his staff:

> This is something I have been pounding on now for over a year — apparently with little success. I have emphasized time and time again the urgent necessity for having perfect team play between Air Support units and Ground troops. I have brought out, and I thought in no unmistakable terms, the fact that this cannot be accomplished without thorough training in communications, in technique, and in procedure.[7]

Most fighter-bomber pilots in the Ninth Air Force received their training in ground attack during operations in Europe. Arnold urged Spaatz to develop "100 percent day and night support for ground forces. Will you keep these tactical requirements in your mind and give General Brereton all required support to build up the Ninth Air Force."[8] Arnold warned Brereton that "the increasing effectiveness of light flak indicates to me that the major part of the low altitude attack burden must fall on your fighters."[9]

With Arnold's prodding, Spaatz and Brereton directed the growth of the most powerful tactical air force ever to fly in battle. The Ninth Air Force gave OVERLORD's American ground forces excellent air support.

Bradley quickly came to appreciate the support the First Army received from the IX Tactical Air Command [IX TAC]. In his postwar book he wrote:

> As a result of our inability to get together with air in England, we went into France almost totally untrained in air-ground cooperation. But we also went in with an offsetting advantage in a breezy young major general named Elwood P. Quesada....

Major General E.P. Quesada (courtesy of USAFHRA).

> He succeeded brilliantly in a task where many airmen before him failed, partly because he was willing to dare anything once. Unlike most airmen who viewed ground support as a bothersome diversion to war in the sky, Quesada approached it as a vast new frontier waiting to be explored.[10]

Although somewhat overstated, and illustrative of the antipathy many ground commanders felt toward airmen, this statement does point out Quesada's innovative spirit. He encouraged his fighter-bomber pilots to find solutions to problems regardless of guidelines. IX TAC adopted new weapons, including high velocity aircraft rockets and napalm. Innovative uses of radar and radio helped pilots bomb and navigate in darkness and bad weather.

Perhaps the most important innovation pioneered by IX TAC was armored column cover. Airmen with VHF radio sets were stationed in tank commands. They communicated with flights of fighter-bombers sent to support the armored force. With their knowledge and experience of fighter operations, they were able to give pilots missions they could execute effectively. This air-ground cooperation worked well and won high praise from ground forces. Pilots often alerted tanks to problems or opportunities.

Brereton frequently reminded his subordinates that mobility was the key to success with a tactical air force. It had to remain close to the army it supported. Flexibility was also crucial. Fighter-bomber groups switched from one tactical air command to another to meet changing conditions. They executed a variety of missions, including air combat, interdiction of enemy transportation, close support of ground forces, reconnaissance, and bomber escort.

As more U.S. armies were formed, new tactical air commands were set up to support them. When the Third Army became operational on August 1, 1944, XIX TAC, commanded by Brigadier General Otto Weyland, was assigned to support it.

```
                    NINTH AIR FORCE
                    Maj. Gen. Hoyt Vandenberg

IX TROOP CARRIER CMD              IX BOMBER CMD
Brig. Gen. Paul Williams          Brig. Gen. Samuel Anderson

IX TACTICAL AIR CMD               XIX TACTICAL AIR CMD
Maj. Gen. Elwood Quesada          Brig. Gen. Otto Weyland

                    IX AIR FORCE SERVICE CMD
                    IX ENGINEER CMD
                    IX AIR DEFENSE CMD
```

Diagram 2. Ninth Air Force

Lieut. General Hoyt Vanderberg (courtesy of USAFHRA).

In the months before D-Day, Brereton ordered his fighter pilots to attack ground targets on their return flights from escorting bombers. Attacks on railroads, airfields, flying bomb launch sites and other ground targets gave pilots experience in ground attack that would pay dividends later. Ground crews learned how to transform fighters into fighter-bombers, and pilots learned how to employ them.

General Brereton led the Ninth Air Force during its first eight months as a part of OVERLORD. In July he was replaced by Lieut. General Hoyt Vandenberg. Although its ground support techniques were not fully developed by D-Day, it was a battle-tested organization. It had participated in the strategic bombing campaign during which the AAF achieved its major objective — air superiority. It also took part in pre–D-Day interdiction of German transportation facilities. After D-Day it had to fine-tune procedures and equipment to give close support to ground forces.

On the eve of D-Day, Brereton reported to Arnold that his two tactical air commands were "completely organized and operational." IX Bomber Command and IX Troop Carrier Command were also ready for D-Day. Brereton commanded the Ninth Air Force during the first critical weeks of the invasion, then became commander of the First Allied Airborn Army.[11]

After five weeks of battle in the hedgerows of the bocage and around Caen, Allied commanders searched for ways to break the virtual stalemate, with its slow progress and high casualty totals. Leigh-Mallory suggested to Eisenhower that the strategic air forces could do more to help the armies. He proposed that heavy bombers drop an enormous "carpet" of bombs on a small sector of the front. This would demoralize, perhaps paralyze, the defenders so that Allied troops could break through the front. With Eisenhower's backing, Leigh-Mallory held firm against protests from the strategic air force commanders. Spaatz derided the proposed operation as one that would merely "plow up several square miles of terrain."

A carpet bombing was executed by RAF Bomber Command on a sector of the British front in July. The results seemed to vindicate Spaatz. British troops gained only a few miles. German soldiers recovered from the bombing much sooner than expected and organized a firm defense.

In spite of this disappointment, plans went forward to execute another carpet bombing on the First Army front. This time American air forces would execute the mission. It would start an offensive called Operation COBRA.

The First Army fought hard to gain ground that could be used to launch COBRA. It entered St. Lô on July 18. This rail and road hub was demolished. American troops called it the "capital of ruins." West of St. Lô was a straight road that Bradley chose as a boundary of the sector to be subjected to a carpet bombing.

COBRA struck on July 25 with an attack by fighter-bombers on a section of the front, one mile by five miles, near St. Lô. Then, 1586 heavy bombers dropped more than 50,000 bombs on the target area. As the last bombs fell, ground troops advanced. German resistance was stronger than anticipated and the first day's gains were meager. That evening, General Collins made a crucial decision. He ordered VII Corps' armor to attack in the morning. This move resulted in the breakthrough that made German positions untenable and permitted Allied forces to drive southward into country better suited to mobile warfare. As German forces abandoned strong defensive positions and moved on roads in daylight, they were attacked by Allied fighter-bombers.

The time was ripe for the Third Army to enter the battle to exploit the enemy's deteriorating situation. Patton had fretted constantly about being on the sidelines during June and July, but his absence from combat served an important Allied deception operation. He performed brilliantly as commander of a fictitious army group in the UK supposedly preparing to invade the Pas de Calais. Germans were led to believe that this operation would employ the major invasion force. They kept sizable forces north of the Seine River to repel it. The Allies' overwhelming air supremacy prevented the Germans from executing aerial reconnaissance to uncover the deceptions.

The Third Army occupied positions on the First Army's right as it made final preparations to attack. Patton told his leading armored units to strike southward toward Avranches, where they would squeeze through a narrow opening between German forces and the sea. The Third Army's primary objectives were ports of Brittany, especially Brest. The lack of ports was one of Eisenhower's greatest worries at this time.

When the Third Army became operational, General Bradley assumed command of the 12th Army Group composed of the First and Third Armies.

As the Third Army's tanks charged through Avranches, no one, not even Patton, could have anticipated that it was the start of one of the most successful offensives of World War II. Seven weeks later, the Third Army would be three hundred miles east of Avranches—within a day's march of the German frontier.

1

Breakthrough into Brittany

The Third Army executed highly mobile operations in August. They required outstanding staff work and flexibility of commanders. Patton expected his subordinates to have initiative and not always be waiting for orders. Commanders of his armored divisions came from the cavalry, a branch which encouraged audacity. Patton's favorite maxim was toujours l'audace. In difficult situations he would remind himself not to take counsel from his fears.

During campaigns in the ETO, a total of forty-two divisions served with the Third Army, with only a few serving for the entire period. Diagram 3 shows the corps assigned to the Third Army in August 1944:

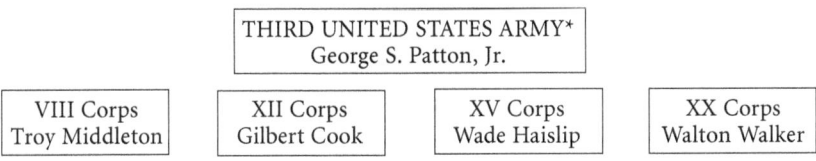

*August 1, 1944

Diagram 3. Third United States Army

In the U.S. Army, the corps had the key headquarters for employing combat elements in various tactical combinations. Corps changed as they gained or lost divisions or other units. A corps commander needed exceptional stamina; his area of responsibility might extend over a front of one hundred miles.

A corps usually had two or more infantry divisions, each with three regiments of about 9500 men, 18 howitzers of 105 mm, 54 anti-tank guns of 57 mm, and 642 vehicles. Division artillery had about 200 men, 375 vehicles, and fired 36 howitzers of 155 mm. Attached to an infantry division were a military police platoon, an ordnance company, a quartermaster company, a signal company, a cavalry reconnaissance troop, an engineer battalion and a medical battalion.[1]

Infantry outfits fought with rifles, bayonets, grenades, mortars, machine guns and pistols. Some soldiers employed flame throwers and bazookas. Bazookas were shouldered tubes which fired rockets with tremendous penetrating power, useful against armored vehicles and fortified positions. A shortage of trained riflemen hampered infantry divisions. Rifle companies suffered the most casualties, and replacements were hard to recruit. Most volunteers tended to choose other military services or other branches of the army, such as artillery, armor, the air forces or units, such as quartermaster, airborne, ordnance, medical, and engineer, which require highly trained personnel. The educational and physical quality of infantrymen tended to be low. Six percent had attended college; twenty-five percent had completed high school. Some were illiterate and some were rejects from other branches and specialized units.

It was a wonder verging on the miraculous that American infantrymen fought as well as they did.[2]

Armored divisions had three tank battalions, each with 2200 men and 251 tanks; and three infantry battalions, each with 3000 men, 600 vehicles, nine anti-tank guns and three 75 mm howitzers. Division artillery had three motorized battalions, each with 1600 men, nine tanks, 54 howitzers of 105 mm and 159 vehicles. Attached to each armored division were an ordnance maintenance battalion, a medical battalion, an engineer battalion, a military police platoon, a signal company and a cavalry reconnaissance squadron.

It was a tremendous task to keep American divisions supplied with gasoline. Their equipment needed regular maintenance and a steady flow of spare parts.

Patton urged his commanders to lead near the front; they should try to be at the critical place at the crucial time. He obeyed this principle himself. In the hot, dusty days of early August the critical place was Avranches. The Third Army had to squeeze through a narrow corridor between German positions and the sea. It was a tricky situation. Patton's jeep, festooned with flags and stars of his rank, a klaxon blaring, threaded through traffic on the crowded roads. He stationed himself at an important crossroads to help military police direct traffic. Patton wanted his troops to see and recognize their leaders. He wore spotless uniforms, a polished helmet, and glistening cavalry boots. Ivory-handled revolvers hung from his belt.

Avranches occupied a bluff overlooking a bay and the famous monastery, Mont St. Michel. Two important highways ran southward toward Brittany. Brilliant Third Army staff work brought units to the bottleneck

1. Breakthrough into Brittany

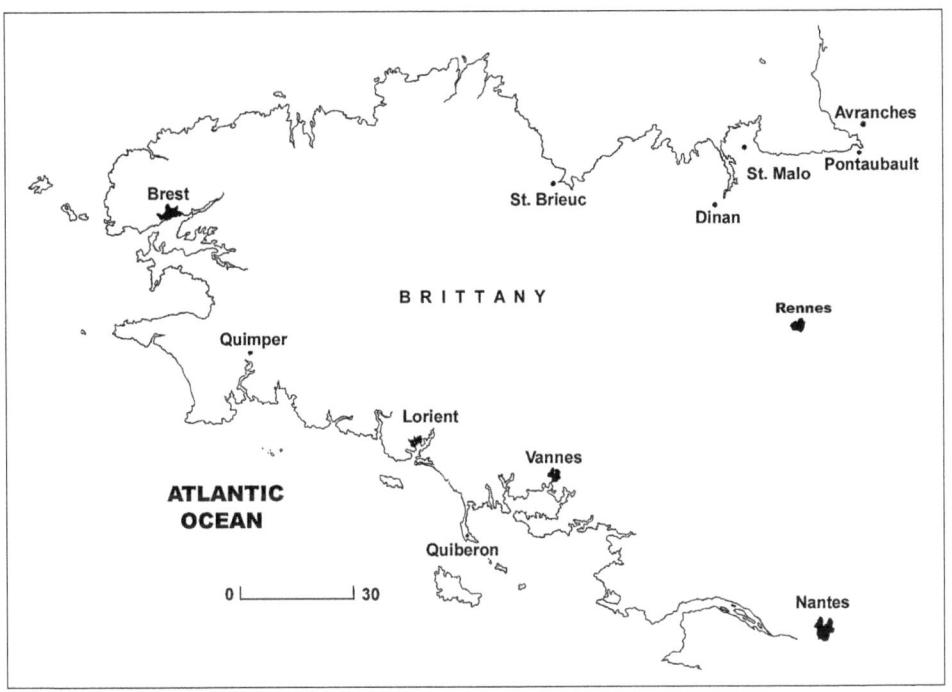

Map 2. Brittany

at precisely the right time. South of Avranches, engineers worked to clear roads, often with sniper bullets ricocheting from their dozer blades.

A few miles south of Avranches a key highway into Brittany crossed a bridge at Pontaubault. Swift movement by the 4th Armored Division secured the bridge before the Germans could demolish it. This became a pattern: the Third Army's speed and surprise often brought it prizes before the enemy could organize defenses for them. For the first few days of the Third Army's operations in Brittany it encountered few organized German units. The situation begged for exploitation, the kind of slashing, driving campaign that armored forces were trained to carry out. The Battle of Normandy had been slow and costly. The Third Army's drive into Brittany opened with speed and exhilarating advances, but all was not smooth and swift. An Army history criticized the campaign: "A confusion of purpose and method ... which was to mar the breakout, stemmed from the abruptness of the change from static to mobile warfare and from the contrasting personalities of the leaders involved."[3] The VIII Corps commander, Major General Troy Middleton, and Bradley tended to be more cautious than Patton.

When the Third Army's armored divisions raced around the German left end into Brittany, they followed established doctrine about their proper employment. Their personnel were exceptionally well-trained and thoroughly indoctrinated in armored operations. For more than two years they had trained in the U.S. and U.K. Their morale was high and they expected to be successful. Their commanders believed their best position was in the enemy's rear, creating havoc with communications and supply systems, and panic among enemy staff and service personnel. The speed and momentum of the tank forces made it difficult for the enemy to establish strong defensive positions. The Third Army commanders believed it was a misuse of armor to allow it to get bogged down in static engagements.

Patton and his armored commanders embraced the doctrine of exploitation, none more wholeheartedly than Maj. General John S. Wood, commander of the 4th Armored Division. In the peacetime Army Wood had been senior to Eisenhower and Bradley, and he rarely hesitated to lecture them about the proper way to run the war. He believed he knew as much about armored operations as any officer, and more than most. Like Patton, Wood commanded from a jeep or puddle-jumper airplane. He had little patience with long-winded briefing sessions.

Wood believed that Allied strategy for operations in Brittany was wrong. Specifically, the 4th Armored should be moving eastward toward Germany, not westward. Like Patton, he believed that battle commanders, not logistics experts, should make military decisions. Wood explained to anyone who would listen that it was wrong to fight for ports in Brittany. They were too far from Germany.

Under Wood's leadership, the 4th Armored Division developed a fighting style based on swift movement and disruption of enemy communications; it tried to avoid getting bogged down in attacks on strong defensive positions.

On August 1 Wood's tanks reached Rennes, a major road and rail hub of Brittany. Combat Command A [CCA] of the 4th Armored Division, led by Colonel Bruce C. Clarke, quickly overcame rather strong enemy resistance. The swift capture of Rennes surprised Middleton, who did not expect it to fall so soon. The capture of Rennes confirmed some of the 4th Armored's guidelines for tank operations. Adaptability was the key to success. Clark concluded that armor could advance on a narrow front and that it could fight in towns.[4]

Behind enemy lines unforeseen situations always develop. Armored

Opposite: **Major General John S. Wood (courtesy of USAMHI).**

American soldiers filling gasoline jerricans (courtesy of USAFHRA).

task forces had to bring enough rations, gasoline and ammunition to permit movement until supply vehicles reached them.

Wood made plans to position his forces around Rennes so that they could move eastward on short notice, as he believed they should. He sent a message to Middleton outlining his intentions. Without waiting for approval, he ordered some of the moves to begin.

Middleton sensed that he and Wood were not clearly in agreement on the Army's main objective, which was to capture some ports in Brittany. Bradley had told Middleton to capture Quiberon on Brittany's southern coast. Handicapped by poor communications, Middleton decided to visit Wood — no easy task, since he had to pass through areas still not clear of German troops. Middleton listened to Wood's arguments for moving east, then told him to leave part of his division near Rennes and to move part of it southwest toward Quibiron.

Patton supported Middleton's decision. He sent the 4th Armored Division to the west and southwest "in accordance with the Army plan."[5]

Wood then sent a combat command to take Vannes on Brittany's southern coast. After a short pause to stock up on gasoline and ammunition, the 4th Armored Division moved toward the important port city of Lorient. Manned by strong forces with plenty of guns, ammunition and tank traps, Lorient would not fall to a swift tank assault. Hitler had declared it to be a "fortress." He ordered the commander to hold it to the last man and last cartridge, and to demolish the port facilities before the last round was fired.

Wood concluded that Lorient was too strong to be taken by a single armored division. He advised Middleton that the 4th Armored should "get ready to hit again in a more profitable direction, namely to Paris." Again Patton sent word to the stubborn Wood to remain in the vicinity of Lorient and await orders. Wood later remarked that this order "was one of the great mistakes of the war." Great opportunities for exploitation by armor lay to the east.[6] Patton understood Wood's frustration, but his hands were tied. With a supply crisis developing, SHAEF wanted ports. Unexpectedly, Middleton sent orders more in line with Wood's hopes. He was to keep forces at Lorient but not get involved in a battle. At the same time he should send a combat command to support infantry at Nantes.

On August 12 a combat command of the 4th Armored Division captured Nantes. Three days later the division was relieved of responsibility for Lorient. Wood gathered his forces for a drive "in the right direction."

Patton felt no more enthusiasm for an offensive in Brittany than Wood, but he could not protest vociferously. Patton was on the OVERLORD team by sufferance. Bradley served under Patton in Sicily and thought him to be too reckless, self-promoting, flamboyant and difficult to direct. Eisenhower debated with himself a long time before giving command of the Third Army to Patton. After widespread complaints about Patton's behavior in slapping a soldier, and speaking out of turn in the U.K. about U.S. policy, doubts arose at SHAEF about Patton's judgment and ability to exercise high command. Eisenhower reprimanded Patton but decided to keep him. Years later Eisenhower explained: "In pursuit and exploitation there is need for a commander who sees nothing but the necessity of getting ahead; the more he drives his men the more he will save their lives." In this statement Ike expressed Patton's basic philosophy of command.[7]

Field Marshal Gunther von Kluge sent a description of the situation in early August: "The enemy air superiority is terrific, and smothers almost every one of our movements. Every movement of the enemy, however, is prepared and protected by its air force. Losses in men and equipment are extraordinary. The morale of the troops has suffered very heavily under

AAF liaison aircraft (courtesy of USAFHRA).

constant murderous enemy fire, especially since all infantry units consist only of haphazard groups which do not form a strongly coordinated force any longer. In the rear areas of the front, terrorists, feeling the end approaching, grow steadily bolder. This fact and the loss of numerous signal installations make an orderly command extremely difficult."[8]

When the Third Army became operational in France on August 1, one of Bradley's first orders to Patton was to capture Brest, a major port two hundred miles west of Avranches. Patton told Major General Robert Grow, commander of the 6th Armored Division, to take Brest and to secure railroad bridges in Brittany. SHAEF hoped to use Brest as a major port for American forces.

Grow did not complain about an order to move in the "wrong direction." It was a mission, he said, "from a cavalryman to a cavalryman." One U.S. Army history suggests that it "might have seemed like madness to … expect a solitary division to drive two hundred miles into enemy territory and single-handedly capture a fortress of unknown strength.…" The 6th Armored Division burst into Brittany to accomplish this task.

Six miles west of Pontaubault, the 6th Armored ran into German forces in well-camouflaged positions. Accurate artillery fire caused a brief delay. On August 2 progress was rapid and virtually unopposed. The next day Grow received a disturbing order from Middleton to attack Dinan and St. Malo. This would delay the 6th Armored's move to Brest and hurt its chances to capture the port before the Germans could build up a strong defense for it. Grow halted his westward drive and organized a task force to move northward to Dinan.

Grow was surprised on the morning of August 4 to see an impressive figure trudging toward him through a wheat field. General Patton's first words rang out clearly: "What the hell are you doing sitting here? I thought I told you to go to Brest."[9]

Grow pulled out the order from Middleton. Patton examined it and told Grow to "go ahead where I told you to go." This incident illustrates the kind of communications problems that bedeviled the Third Army in August. Orders canceling missions arrived too late. Messages from divisions to corps and army headquarters acknowledged orders that had been changed. Patton had to overrule his corps commanders at times. Without reliable telephone, teletype or radio communications, corps and army headquarters staff were often uncertain about the location or intentions of the Third Army's armored divisions. Patton asked XIX TAC to carry out extensive aerial reconnaissance to help him keep informed about his forces. Commanders used small liaison airplanes to visit subordinates and to carry important messages and personnel.

Grow sent a message to Middleton: "pursuant to verbal orders [from] Army Commander [we] bypassed Dinan ... proceeding S. and W." Middleton, Grow and Patton eventually came to understand each other's intentions. Bradley sometimes bypassed Patton and gave directions to corps commanders. He told Middleton that he wanted St. Malo, even if this caused a delay in taking Brest.[10]

After several days of rapid movement, including a night march, the 6th Armored arrived in the vicinity of Brest. Grow sent a request for help. His troops could "live off the country" for rations, but gasoline and ammunition had to be sent to him from army stores. Patton promised to send the supplies and troops the 6th Armored needed.

No one in the 12th Army Group knew how strong German defenses at Brest were. Some garrisons surrendered after a show of force, others defended their positions with skill and tenacity. Grow hoped to capture Brest without heavy fighting. On August 8 he sent an ultimatum to the Brest commander asking for surrender of the garrison in the face of "overwhelming forces." This bluff was promptly rejected.[11]

In the next few days, probing attacks showed clearly that Brest would be taken only by tough fighting involving heavy artillery, infantry assaults, demolitions by engineer units, and strong air support. Middleton agreed with this judgment. He sent a message to Grow: "I believe it unwise to become too involved in a fight at Brest.... Watch the situation and wait until an infantry division arrives. Heavy artillery will arrive with the infantry division." Middleton was then preoccupied by an attempt to take St. Malo. On August 12 he ordered Grow to send part of the 6th Armored to Lorient to relieve the 4th Armored Division.[12]

The 6th Armored Division had failed to take Brest, but it had cleared a large part of Brittany, and by so doing created conditions favorable to irregular operations of the French Resistance. Grow believed that the Brittany campaign of the 6th Armored supported U.S Army doctrine for armored operations. Tanks should be mobile and employed with speed and audacity.

Despite its long period of training, the 6th Armored Division made some surprising mistakes in the Brittany campaign. Tank-infantry coordination was poor; small German units delayed large armored forces for long periods; tanks tended to be road-bound; traffic jams were not promptly cleared; infantry spent too much time in ditches.[13]

Allied supply and naval services overcame tremendous obstacles to support the Third Army in Brittany. Ships and even small craft brought ammunition and fuel to small ports on the north coast.

No one can ever know if Brest could have been taken by the 6th Armored division had it not been delayed by an aborted attack on Dinan. French Resistance leaders told Grow that Brest would have fallen to him if he had arrived a few days sooner before German reinforcements reached the city.

Hitler's "fortress" strategy was working. German garrisons held ports the Allies needed, such as Brest, St. Malo, Lorient, St. Nazaire, Le Havre and Boulogne. Before they surrendered, Germans would demolish port facilities. The critical condition of the Allies' supply situation caused Bradley to order Middleton to take St. Malo, even though it was not a major port.

Third Army's rapid drive into Brittany in early August put unexpected pressure on Allied supply lines. Military goods were stockpiled in large quantities in the U.K., U.S., and aboard cargo ships waiting to unload. Cherbourg and the Normandy beaches handled most Allied cargo. Lack of ports was a serious constriction in supply lines. In August it was already assuming the proportions of a calamity. Beach unloading used improvised harbors and docks. Storms caused interruptions in their operations.

Bradley decided that St. Malo's garrison should not be bypassed. Its

American soldiers fighting in St. Malo (courtesy of USAMHI).

guns threatened ships using the port of Granville near Avranches. Middleton organized a task force to drive along Brittany's north shore to secure harbors and railway bridges. He ordered the 83rd Infantry Division to take St. Malo.

Built on a rocky coast, the ancient fortified city of St. Malo had stone walls twenty to thirty feet high. The garrison had constructed underground chambers with living quarters and supply rooms. Artillery weapons projected through armored portholes to cover land and sea approaches. Antiaircraft guns, protected by steel and concrete, fired from the walls. The heart of the fortress was the Citadel, located on a rocky promontory.

German heavy artillery units occupied the island of Cézembre, three miles offshore. Their guns could fire on forces attacking St. Malo and ships using the Bay Mont St. Michel.

Attacks by the 83rd Division on St. Malo's fortifications began on August 9. Artillery pounded a thick-walled chateau in the town. Several pillboxes were wiped out. Allied air forces launched the first of many attacks. The results were disappointing. Infantry charged into the town on August 14. After prolonged, bitter street-fighting, most of St. Malo came under American control, except for the Citadel.

B-26s bombing in French hedgerow country (courtesy of NARA).

Major General Robert C. Macon, commander of the 83rd Division, tried a number of tactical moves to convince the Germans to surrender, including subterranean explosives, and psychological warfare. He arranged to have the German commander's French mistress appeal to him to give up a lost cause. Artillery pounded the Citadel, but a shortage of shells developed. Air attacks by fighter, medium and even heavy bombers tried to shatter the defenders' positions and morale.

The garrison in the town surrendered on August 17. The 83rd Division captured over ten thousand prisoners.

Troops on the island of Cézembre refused to surrender. Middleton and Bradley agreed that the island would have to be taken. P-38 fighter-bombers hit it with napalm — jellied gasoline carried in droptanks. Heavy bombers attacked the island. Naval guns also pounded the fortifications. IX Bomber Command struck the island on the night of August 6/7 and returned three more times. RAF Bomber Command also bombed it.[14]

On September 2, as infantry climbed into boats to invade the island, a white flag appeared over the enemy positions. The Germans' water supply had run out.

St. Malo's commander told Allied interrogators that artillery fire knocked out guns in the town. This forced him to surrender. Air attacks were not decisive or even a major factor in the final capitulation of the fortress. Napalm had little impact on German troops. He claimed that the defenders had only rifles and bayonets to fight with at the end.

The Ninth Bomber Command had sent B-26 medium bombers to attack St. Malo's fortifications. The B-26 was a single-winged, two-engined aircraft with a crew of six. It was effective against air fields, bridges, flying-bomb installations, railroad centers, troop concentrations, supply storage sites, and vehicle parks. It did little decisive damage, however, to fortified positions such as St. Malo. On missions to cut transportation facilities behind German lines, medium bombers usually flew at altitudes between 10,000 and 14,000 feet, where flak was less deadly than at lower altitudes. If the target was important enough, mediums sometimes attacked under cloud cover, usually at about 4000 feet, sometimes even lower. Often the mediums were escorted by fighters. Medium bombers could carry four 1000-pound bombs, two 2000-pound bombs or a variety of bomb loads made up of smaller bombs. To give a reasonable probability of hitting relatively small targets, medium bomb groups had to employ formations of at least 18 aircraft. The Ninth Air Force guidelines warned: "To employ this weapon against targets too heavy to be damaged or too light to justify 36 tons of bombs is a waste of power."[15] The B-26 was vulnerable to fighters and flak.

A-20 hit by flak (courtesy of NARA).

During the Battle of France, the A-20 Havoc was the principal light bomber of the Ninth Air Force. A two-engined monoplane with a crew of three or four, the A-20 was designed for low-level attack, but flak in the ETO made this impractical. It carried six bombs but none larger than 500 pounds. The A-20's excellent pilot visibility made it useful in night operations.[16]

By September 2, when Cézembre surrendered, the Third Army had cleared most of Brittany. Two of its corps were driving toward the Seine. Allied forces had landed on French shores of the Mediterranean. VIII Corps would soon be assigned to the Ninth U.S. Army. Rumors spread that the war would soon be over. German forces still occupied Lorient, St. Nazaire and Brest. They did not always obey Hitler's order to fight to the last man, but they held on to some ports until the war's end. Those ports that surrendered were usually demolished first.

The Ninth Air Force Operational Research Section [ORS] hurriedly prepared a report on air operations in support of the offensive against St. Malo. It found that the bombing attacks on the fort were "without effect." Concluding that fortifications such as those at St. Malo were not

	B-26	**A-20**
Maximum bomb load	4000 pounds	2000 pounds
Ceiling	14,000 feet	15,000 feet
Armament	12 machine guns	9 machine guns
Speed	200 mph	225 mph
Rate of climb	300 feet per min.	1150 feet per min.
Endurance	4.5 hours	2.5 hours

(A change in one or more of these characteristics could bring about changes in others. For example, a reduction in bomb load could make possible a greater speed or endurance. Later models of the A-20 could carry up to 4000 pounds of bombs.)

Table 1. Ninth Air Force Medium and Light Bombers

suitable targets for bombing, ORS analysts hoped that its report would discourage misuse of Ninth Air Force resources in future. In this they were disappointed. The Ninth Air Force received orders to give Brest its highest priority.

French Resistance groups gave valuable help to the Third Army in Brittany. They protected railroad lines and bridges, contained German forces in pockets of resistance, provided guides for VIII Corps units, and cleared Germans from some areas bypassed by the Third Army.[17] Their greatest value came from the intelligence they provided about German forces—their locations, size, weapons and morale. Third Army soldiers quickly learned to appreciate and exploit the resources of the Resistance.

Lack of arms was a major Resistance weakness. General Middleton promised the French that they could have captured German weapons and equipment, but they had to turn over German prisoners to VIII Corps. When negotiating surrender terms, Germans always insisted that they become prisoners of the U.S. Army. Given this assurance they surrendered sooner. American treatment of prisoners of war followed general U.S. Army policies. The French complained that the Allies treated German prisoners better than Resistance fighters. Before D-Day SHAEF was unsure about what to expect from Resistance actions. It assumed they would be useful, but not something that could be counted on and put into battle plans. Nevertheless, steps were taken to assist Resistance groups. The Eighth Air Force launched a major campaign to supply the Resistance. Allied agents parachuted into Brittany in August to organize landing grounds and reception teams for supplies flown to the Resistance from the U.K.

The speed and power of Third Army operations in Brittany disrupted German forces and set up many opportunities for Resistance actions.

During VIII Corps operations that cleared the north shore, Resistance groups helped Americans take many small towns and ports.

Despite severe shortages of arms and equipment, the French achieved remarkable victories. Nevertheless, there were many disappointments and tragedies that occurred when they attempted tasks beyond their resources.

An American officer working with the French related an interesting tale. He had parachuted into Brittany to arrange for the destruction of twelve bridges. None of these bridges were blown. As it turned out, this "failure" helped U.S. forces move more rapidly. Throughout August, blown bridges hurt the Third Army more than they helped.[18]

The Resistance had some Monday-morning quarterbacks, and their complaints have found their way into many histories. Typical of these is the claim that Americans could have taken Lorient if only they had followed the advice of Resistance leaders.[19]

Throughout the years of the German occupation, the Resistance was treated brutally. When captured, members faced torture and summary executions. Civilians were taken hostage, sometimes executed, and some towns were destroyed in punishment for what the Germans called "terrorist actions." When their turn came, the French sometimes treated German prisoners harshly. After Brittany was liberated, a period of upheaval ensued. Neither American nor French authorities could prevent all acts of vengeance against the Germans and the French who had collaborated with them during four years of occupation.

In September most of Brittany, other than a few ports, was cleared of German forces. The French administered civilian and military affairs under the authority of the French Provisional Government, headed by General Charles de Gaulle. This freed American troops for operations in eastern France.

Patton established good relations with the French under his command. He had many friends in the French officer corps. He had served in France during World War I, traveled extensively in the country, attended its cavalry school, and spoke the language. He understood French sensitivity about their defeat in 1940. Many French leaders felt that Americans did not treat them with the respect they had earned. Some of this antipathy emanated from de Gaulle, who distrusted American leaders and was constantly embroiled in quarrels with them.[20]

With a flexibility that the AAF had promised if given autonomy, XIX TAC switched priorities from destruction of transportation facilities to disrupt enemy movements (interdiction), to close support of ground forces. XIX TAC's responsibilities increased with every mile gained by the

Third Army. The Ninth Air Force increased the number of fighter-bomber and reconnaissance squadrons assigned to XIX TAC.

General Patton established a ground rule that the AAF had been slow in adopting. He wanted interdiction executed in concert with ground operations. In some cases it would be valuable to block German offensives or retreats. In other situations it was important to keep the Third Army's path clear. This policy required close cooperation between Patton, Vandenberg and Weyland and their staffs. On August 1, as Patton's forces roared along roads south of Avranches, XIX TAC assigned two of its groups to cover the Third Army's armored columns. A third group flew armed reconnaissance in front of the tanks.

In August, one part of the Third Army began an assault on Brest. Simultaneously, XV and XX Corps drove southeastward toward the Loire River. Targets were scattered, and many were attacked as "targets of opportunity" by XIX TAC's pilots, who were learning to spot targets and how to attack them.

2

The Ninth Air Force

XIX Tactical Air Command [XIX TAC] was assigned to give close air support to the Third Army. XIX TAC's fighter-bomber groups had combat-tested personnel, equipment, tactics and procedures. Most of its groups flew P-47 Thunderbolts. This airplane, originally designed as a high-altitude fighter, had served the Eighth Air Force as an escort for heavy bombers during the battles for air superiority of 1943 and 1944. In fact, many XIX TAC P-47s had come from the Eighth Air Force. During the pre-invasion buildup of the Ninth Air Force in the U.K., XIX TAC's groups executed ground attack missions against airfields, railroads, bridges, and flying-bomb launch sites. After D-Day, XIX TAC executed a variety of ground attack missions in support of Allied ground forces.

Fighter-Bomber Groups	*Aircraft*
36	P-47
354	P-51
358	P-47
362	P-47
363	P-51
371	P-47
373	P-47
405	P-47
406	P-47

Table 2. XIX TACTICAL AIR COMMAND, August-September 1944

Brigadier General Otto P. Weyland took command of XIX TAC in February 1944 when it was known as an Air Support Command. Weyland was born in Riverside, California, on January 27, 1902. His father, a pacifist, had fled from Germany to avoid induction into the German army. Weyland graduated from Texas A & M in 1923 and enlisted in the Army Air Service a year later. At the start of World War II, Weyland commanded a

2. The Ninth Air Force   35

P-47 taking off with bombs in wing racks (courtesy of NARA).

Major General O. P. Weyland (courtesy of NARA).

fighter group. Before coming to the U.K. in 1944 to command XIX TAC, he served as an assistant to General Arnold. Weyland later recalled that he was Arnold's favorite whipping boy.

Patton, himself a pilot, described the relationship between the Third Army and XIX TAC as "love at first sight." In England in the months before D-Day, Patton and Weyland became friends. They agreed that Weyland ran his air command free of interference from Patton or his staff. XIX TAC was not a subordinate part of the Third Army. This reflected general U.S. Army doctrine that land power and air power are co-equal and independent forces. Neither is an auxiliary of the other.[1] Weyland's immediate superior was Major General Hoyt Vandenberg, commander of the Ninth Air Force. Vandenberg was subordinate to the AEAF commander, Leigh-Mallory, and General Spaatz, commander of USSTAF. Spaatz did not hesitate to bypass AEAF and give direction to the Ninth Air Force.

In the peacetime regular Army, Vandenberg had specialized in fighter operations. He had taught classes in aerial combat at the Air Corps Tactical School. During his tenure as deputy commander of AEAF, Vandenberg had followed Eisenhower's advice to "protect American interests." He became commander of the Ninth Air Force when Brereton was picked to command the First Allied Airborne Army [FAAA].

In an interview, Weyland stated that he ran XIX TAC without interference from Patton:

> There could be no misunderstanding about it. I had full control of the air. The decisions were mine as to how I would allocate the air effort. And we had a joint operations center with staff officers from his forces....
>
> We would try to support him, but we had other chores to do like maintaining [air] superiority, interdiction to the rear to clobber reserves, ammunition, supplies and things like that ... or perhaps helping out somebody else or doing something that General Eisenhower directed as a joint effort of all the air power.[2]

Weyland's summary of XIX TAC's priorities merely restated those of the AAF. Number one was air superiority. This was achieved by Allied air forces, principally the U.S. Eighth Air Force, in air battles over Germany in 1943–44. It was part of the Allied strategic bombing campaigns. The assault on the German oil industry, executed in 1944, had a profound impact on Germany's ability to wage war. Fuel shortages handicapped German forces and industries. When the GAF fought to curtail Allied strategic bombing, it lost many of its experienced pilots. During the Battle of

France the GAF was too weak to seriously threaten Allied invasion forces. Air supremacy gave Allied ground forces tremendous advantages.

The AAF gave second priority to interdiction of the battlefield. Interdiction interfered with transportation of enemy troops, equipment and supplies into or within the battle area. The Ninth Air Force expended a large share of its effort on interdiction. From March 1 to D-Day, IX Bomber Command made thirty-six attacks against railroad marshalling yards. Analysis of these attacks showed that they were not as effective as planners hoped they would be. German authorities quickly rounded up French civilians to repair lines within 24 to 48 hours. Traffic was interrupted for only a short time.[3]

In May, Allied air forces had started a campaign to destroy bridges on the Seine River. This effort was successful. By D-Day every railroad bridge and most road bridges on the Seine between Paris and the Channel were cut. The German director of military transportation later reported that bridge destruction gave him major problems.[4] After D-Day the bridge campaign was extended to the Loire River, with excellent results. Blocked bridges forced German troops moving to Normandy to make long detours. They tended to bunch up on approaches to the few remaining river crossings, where they were attacked repeatedly by fighter-bombers. These roundabout road marches wore out treads on armored vehicles, created maintenance problems, and consumed dwindling supplies of fuel. Most importantly, German reinforcements arrived at the beachhead too late and too disorganized to repel Allied invasion forces.

Track cuts were another interdiction tactic. They had several advantages: tracks could be cut in areas with little or no flak defenses, and where civilian labor was not plentiful. IX TAC's commander, General Quesada, wrote about interdiction to a friend:

> I am quite proud of our ability to cut railroad tracks and destroy bridges with a minimum number of sorties. We can keep the railroads in any one area cut by dispatching small flights to various points, ramming bombs into the embankment from low level.... If you cut the track in approximately four places at any one time, it is necessary for him [Germans] to repair the cuts one at a time as he can't move his equipment to the middle area.[5]

With overwhelming air superiority, Allied air forces could concentrate on programs of interdiction. The greatest problems with such programs were darkness and cloud cover. German forces were compelled to move at night or in periods of bad weather. In daytime they concealed themselves in forests and with clever camouflage materials. The Ninth Air

Force tried to disrupt German night operations by dropping delayed action bombs at crossroads and by attacking positions in the light of flares. Neither tactic was very effective. Quesada wrote that, "In this theater, we have him stopped cold during the daylight, however, the German is very expert at night movement and concealment.... I have made some effort to become more effective during the hours of darkness, however, our efforts are in reality feeble.... I don't quite know why we haven't developed a long burning flare...."[6] The tactical air commands sometimes cut tracks late in the day so that repair efforts were complicated by darkness.

The extraordinary effectiveness of the Ninth Air Force in the Battle of France was made possible largely on AAF victories won long before D-Day. Because the GAF was a thoroughly beaten force during the Allied invasion, the Ninth Air Force could concentrate on support for ground forces, almost free from threats of interference by enemy aircraft. The First and Third Armies could dispense with most of the precautions that ground forces normally take against air attacks, and which consume vast amounts of effort.

From D-Day to the end of the Battle of France, fighter-bombers operated from air strips only a few miles behind front lines. Some analysts, including Brereton and Quesada, believed that fighter-bombers "saved the day" during the Allied landings at Omaha Beach.[7] Allied fighter-bombers bombed and strafed German troops, artillery positions, supply stockpiles and motor vehicles, especially tanks of the powerful Panzer divisions. They also bombed and strafed trains, road traffic, railroad tracks, tunnels, rail centers and bridges. Ninth Air Force reconnaissance pilots brought valuable information to Allied commanders. They also adjusted artillery fire (gave gunners information about the location of shell bursts) and reported the locations of important enemy troop and armor concentrations. Liaison aircraft carried out many different kinds of missions. Transport aircraft flew supply missions, evacuated wounded soldiers, and carried airborne troops into battle. These and many more activities vulnerable to air attack operated with great freedom because of Allied air supremacy.

German artillery and mortar crews often suspended fire if Allied fighter-bombers were overhead. They had to operate without spotter aircraft.

Most Allied activities were eased by air superiority. Allied airfields, command headquarters, stockpiles and fuel dumps were rarely threatened by the German Air Force. Allied vehicles moved freely on roads in daylight, and with headlights on at night. Allied ground forces spent little time and energy in defensive activities that tend to exhaust troops—digging foxholes and trenches, building bunkers, camouflaging positions, lug-

C-47 transport aircraft (courtesy of USAFHRA).

ging supplies long distances. German soldiers had to do many of these tasks at night.

Few Allied tanks were lost to air attacks, whereas enemy armor was a favorite target for Allied fighter-bombers. This was a crucial advantage because German tanks were generally superior to American tanks. German armor often remained immobile in daylight or moved on poorer, secondary roads to avoid detection. Americans used main highways. They had large white stars on their vehicles and colored panels to help airmen identify them as friendly.

A few Allied units learned about air attacks not from the enemy but from Allied aircraft that bombed or strafed them. These accidents were most likely to occur when heavy bombers tried to bomb close to front lines. They were not equipped for close air support, nor were their crews trained for it. Airmen, including the deputy supreme commander of OVERLORD, hated to see heavy bombers employed in close support of ground troops. They argued that such employment made ground commanders become "addicted" to it. If one ground unit attacked a position with strong heavy bomber support and lost only a few men, other units demanded the same help.[8]

Each advantage that air supremacy gave to Allied troops was matched

Damaged Panther tank (courtesy of NARA).

by a corresponding handicap it inflicted on German forces. The Germans had to expend enormous effort on cover and concealment of stockpiles and troop positions. They moved supplies and reinforcements during the brief summer hours of darkness. To protect themselves from air attack, they had to dig elaborate underground shelters. Many of them fought in an exhausted condition, short of fuel and ammunition. Allied bombs and artillery often damaged German communications equipment. German commanders had difficulty sending messages to their troops. They could not travel safely in daylight to visit them. German ground forces expended much effort on antiaircraft operations. Some German commanders, including Field Marshal Rommel, were badly wounded by air attacks. Rommel's successor, Field Marshal von Kluge, was out of touch with both superiors and subordinates for twenty-four hours at a critical time after his vehicle was hit by fighter-bombers. Soon after this incident, Hitler relieved him of his command. The GAF could not operate from airfields near front lines. Many of their fighter squadrons flew from bases east of Paris.

The virtues of air supremacy were fully understood by AAF leaders. They gave top priority to achieving and retaining it.

In the three weeks after the Allied breakout from the beachhead in late July, the Ninth Air Force flew 6000 medium and light bomber sorties, and 20,000 fighter-bomber sorties. Large amounts of German supplies and equipment were destroyed, including 5000 motor vehicles, 105 aircraft, 1600 railroad cars, 650 tanks, 100 locomotives, 32 bridges, and 24 ammunition and fuel depots. Fighter-bombers cut rail tracks in many places.

The AAF gave third priority to close air support to ground forces. This subject is explored in the next chapter.

3

Close Air Support

Many Ninth Air Force fighter pilots were experienced in combat, and many had attacked targets on the ground in the pre-invasion period. But they had to develop effective techniques for giving close support to ground troops. Air and ground staff learned to work together at various headquarters. Air Liaison Officers [ALO] were assigned to division, corps and combat command headquarters. They advised commanders on all matters related to air operations. They evaluated targets proposed by ground forces. Many ALOs were fighter pilots. They could communicate clearly with pilots assigned to fly cover for ground units. Pilots and artillery units worked together. Artillery marked targets for air attack with smoke shells; pilots adjusted artillery fire, something that pre-war doctrine taught them not to do. As cooperation improved, ALOs acted as air controllers for flights that gave them air cover.[1]

Effective air-ground cooperation depended on reliable communications. Telephone, teletype, radio, and couriers served to keep all interested parties informed about operations. The success of a mission usually depended on cooperation between many units. Good communications made it possible to act quickly to attack targets while they were vulnerable or an obstacle to ground units. Occasionally, airmen assigned to one mission were given orders to undertake another, more important, assignment. Missions could be cancelled by radio, thereby avoiding blunders such as air attacks on towns already captured or bridges that would soon be needed by Allied troops. Air-ground communication helped prevent mishaps in which Allied aircraft attacked friendly forces.

Ground forces provided personnel to serve as Ground Liaison Officers [GLO] at headquarters of groups, air commands and air forces. They briefed pilots on situations of ground units. They maintained bomb lines on operations maps. Air attacks on targets between front lines and bomb lines were forbidden, unless clear radio contact had been established with ALOs on the ground. Intelligence officers interviewed pilots after a mission, and information gleaned was disseminated to all who needed it.[2]

XIX TAC pilots visiting a Third Army tank crew (couresy of NARA).

It is remarkable that air and ground liaison parties functioned as well as they did. Tables of organization did not provide personnel for such units. Their training had to be accomplished on the job. They were usually rotated from this assignment after a short time. Before they left, they worked for a few days with their replacements to show them procedures.

Armored column cover was one of the most successful innovations. Some fourteen tanks in each armored division carried the same type of radio set used by fighter-bombers. A fighter pilot rode in a tank of each combat command, with radio equipment to communicate with pilots flying cover. The system worked smoothly. ALOs directed pilots to targets, and pilots called attention to potential problems and opportunities confronting the armored forces. TACs assigned four fighter-bombers to cover armored columns whenever possible.

Weyland recalled that his fighter-bombers often performed tasks normally assigned to artillery: "Here, they were moving, so by the time they'd stopped a column and deployed their artillery and what-not ... hell, it might take them an hour or two. I'd have fighter-bombers out in front, and we'd try to take care of anything out there."[3]

Close air support of ground forces was costly, greatly in demand and limited in availability. One of the principal tasks of ALOs was to evaluate requests for air support. They approved only those which were suitable for air forces and important enough to justify the effort. In fact, evaluation of target requests took place at all levels, and worked smoothly after air and ground officers came to understand each other's needs and capabilities. Often, target requests had to be rejected because the Ninth Air Force was engaged on other missions. This was a sore point with ground personnel.

With Weyland and Quesada working closely together, XIX TAC and IX TAC developed tested techniques and procedures for close air support. The Third Army and XIX TAC worked out effective methods of cooperation in mobile operations.

During clear weather in August, XIX TAC executed an extraordinary number of sorties. Its proficiency in ground attack improved rapidly.

Patton often attended XIX TAC's evening planning sessions. He studied reconnaissance photographs carefully. Weyland and Patton sometimes drove to front lines together. Patton's jeep flew a large four-star flag and had the loudest klaxon Weyland had ever heard. They returned to headquarters more quietly. Patton believed in showmanship. He wanted his troops to see their commander going forward, not back.[4]

Fighter-bomber groups preferred to use 500-pound general-purpose bombs with contact fuses. Sometimes they dropped bombs into smoke from exploding artillery shells. Troops claimed this was effective, but Weyland had doubts about it. The degree of trust that airmen placed in evaluations of air support by ground troops varied. Ground personnel were not as concerned as airmen about waste of resources such as bombs, bullets, rockets, and gasoline, along with wear on aircraft and pilots.

Model	*Bomb Load*	*Tactical Radius*
P-38	2 × 500 pounds	260 miles
	1 × 1000 pounds*	400 miles
	2 × 1000 pounds	250 miles
P-47	2 × 500 pounds	260 miles
	2 × 1000 pounds†	230 miles
P-51	2 × 500 pounds	325 miles

*With one 165-gallon droptank
†With one 108-gallon droptank

Table 3. Bomb Loads and Tactical Radii of Fighter-Bombers

In a postwar interview, Quesada explained the relationship between tactical air commands and ground units: "Bradley was not my commander. My boss theoretically and organizationally was Brereton. So Bradley never did attempt to be my commander. He recognized quite early that we had the ability to use air power in a way that would help him, that he himself could not originate. He recognized clearly that we had a knowledge of our arm that he did not have."[5]

The Ninth Air Force's closest air support was given by fighter-bombers. They were modified P-47s, P-51s and P-38s. These AAF fighters had been designed for high-altitude air combat. For ground attack they had to be modified to have:

1. A tactical radius of not less than 350 miles.*
2. A bomb-carrying capacity of not less than 1000 pounds.
3. Good low-altitude performance.[6]

It soon became evident that of the three fighters, the P-47 was most adaptable for ground attack. It became the best fighter-bomber. It carried bombs or droptanks on racks under its wings and fuselage. It had an endurance of 2 hours and 20 minutes without external tanks, and a bomb-carrying capacity up to 2500 pounds. (Quesada claimed that it could carry three 1000-pound bombs if the runway surface was solid and the tires were pumped up to maximum air pressure.) At low altitude it was less maneuverable than either the P-51 or P-38, but it was least vulnerable to ground fire, the biggest danger to fighter-bombers. Even when its radial air-cooled engine suffered a direct hit it often continued to power the aircraft with whole cylinders shot away. One XIX TAC pilot remembered that P-47s returned from missions "shot to pieces—cylinders blown completely off engines streaming oil, great rents and holes blasted through wings, fuselage and tail planes."[7]

The P-47 Republic Thunderbolt first appeared in the European Theater in early 1943 for service as a high-altitude fighter with the Eighth Air Force. Compared to the finest British and German fighters, it was huge. To maintain engine power at high altitudes, it had a massive supercharger. Its engine developed 2000 horsepower and gave it speeds in excess of 400 miles per hour at 27,000 feet. It carried eight .50 caliber machine guns that could focus a devastating amount of firepower on a wide range of targets. A slow rate of climb limited its usefulness as an interceptor. The engine burned gasoline at a prodigious rate, which gave it a short tactical

---

*Tactical radius is the maximum distance an aircraft can fly away from its base with a normal combat load and return without refueling.

Ground crew loading bombs in wing racks (courtesy of NARA).

radius. This was a major reason why the Eighth Air Force replaced them with P-51s. The P-47's short tactical radius created serious problems when the Third Army raced far ahead of XIX TAC's airfields in France.[8]

P-47 pilots compensated for poor forward visibility by rocking the aircraft. It had a high rate of acceleration in dives. Pilots began dives at altitudes too high for light flak to be effective — 6000 to 8000 feet. They dove at an angle between 25 and 40, degrees and released bombs between 3500 and 1500 feet. To hit critical objectives, P-47 pilots sometimes flew their bombs close to targets. This tactic required bombs with delay fuses. The Thunderbolt's poor rate of climb made the getaway zoom an especially hazardous period.[9]

A few squadrons had P-47s equipped to fire 5-inch high-velocity rockets. Rockets were reputed to be deadly tank destroyers. They had little recoil force when fired.

The P-51 Mustang was designed by the North American Aviation Company of Inglewood, California. It began combat operations with the RAF as a ground attack aircraft. Pilots soon recognized that the Mustang was an excellent fighter, but it lacked an effective supercharger. To improve high altitude performance, Mustangs were fitted with Rolls-Royce Merlin

P-51 with droptanks in wing racks (courtesy of NARA).

engines. By increasing fuel storage capacity and using droptanks, the Mustang became a superb long-range fighter, perhaps the best of World War II. Its tactical radius was phenomenal. With droptanks it could escort heavy bombers to all parts of Germany. The P-51 excelled in aerial combat. It destroyed many GAF fighters in the strategic bombing campaigns.

The P-51 was not a superior ground attack aircraft. It did not have the size, power or strength to carry bombs larger than 500 pounds efficiently. Its liquid-cooled engine was vulnerable to flak. It gave valuable service to the Ninth Air Force on reconnaissance and bomber escort missions.[10]

The P-38 Lightning was a big, two-engine fighter, easily recognized by conical booms extending from its engines to its tail assembly. It carried four .50 caliber machine guns and a 20 mm cannon. Pilots occupied a pod between the engines. The P-38 had a long tactical radius and good low-altitude maneuverability, but its liquid-cooled engines, like those of P-51s, were vulnerable to ground fire. It could, however, fly with one engine at a speed of 300 miles per hour, with its tactical radius barely reduced. In aerial combat, P-38 groups suffered heavy losses to the more maneuverable German fighters. P-38s made valuable contributions to the

P-38 in flight over wreckage of a German airplane (courtesy of NARA).

Ninth Air Force on photographic reconnaissance and special bombing missions, including night bombing using radar. P-38s could carry two 1000-pound bombs without difficulty. Pilot visibility to the front was good, but the wings blocked side views downward.[11] German prisoners reported that P-38s caused them more concern than other fighters.

The striking power and high rate of fire of the P-38's .50 caliber machine guns and its cannon made it a highly destructive weapon, both in aerial combat and ground attack. In the Battle of France it devastated locomotives, military transport, vehicles of all types, artillery, machine gun and anti-aircraft positions, ammunition and fuel dumps, lightly constructed buildings, and troops.

When German forces retreated across France, often stalled in traffic jams, fighter-bombers of the Ninth Air Force destroyed many of their vehicles and killed or wounded many soldiers.

Fighter-bombers had a crew of one, thus pilot recruitment, training and replacement of losses were minimized.

Against heavily armored vehicles the .50 caliber machine gun did little damage, although some success was achieved with bullets that entered air vents or bounced from road surfaces into the bottoms of the vehicles.

The basic unit of fighter-bomber formations was the four-plane flight made up of two elements. The element leaders flew 75 to 100 yards apart, and each had a wing man off to the side 50 to 75 yards. In a sixteen-plane squadron formation, four flights were divided into two sections. The two flights in the "red" section flew in a line abreast, from 200 to 300 yards apart; the two flights of the "blue" section flew 300 yards behind and 500 to 1000 feet higher.[12]

Among the principal advantages of fighter-bombers were their rapid turnarounds, assuming their airfields were not too far from the front. Because of their speed and the short time required for refueling and rearming, a fighter could execute as many as five sorties a day.

The bomb load of fighter-bombers compared favorably with that of light and medium bombers. One man in one airplane could deliver two thousand pounds of bombs. The medium bomber with a crew of six usually carried about four thousand pounds. Fighter-bombers required less manpower for maintenance and service than medium bombers. Fighters could operate from short runways or even grass surfaces, something larger aircraft could not always do.

Medium bomber groups preferred to have at least twenty-four hours to plan a mission, whereas fighter-bombers often responded to calls for help in less than an hour. Bombing accuracy of fighter-bombers was far better than that of heavy and medium bombers, despite simplicity of sighting methods. They could release bombs close to targets.

When a definite target was identified prior to take-off, and planning time was available, pilots studied all available information about it, including maps and photographs of the target area.

When dive-bombing, fighter-bomber pilots preferred to approach targets out of the sun. Planes peeled off in a string, throttling back if necessary to prevent excessive speed. Pilots planned to recover from dives at a minimum of 1000 feet. Normally aircraft pulled out in a climbing turn to regain altitude as quickly as possible, although on many occasions it was safer to remain close to the ground to avoid flak.

Glide bombing was often executed on targets where range errors were relatively unimportant, when cloud cover precluded a dive-bombing attack, or when targets were not heavily defended by antiaircraft artillery. Bombs were released at about 800 feet. Speed was essential to avoid ground fire. The attack was made along the longest dimension of the target because of a high probability of range errors.

Minimum-altitude bombing was done from tree-top level. This kind of bombing was effective against targets with a relatively soft, upright surface to stop and contain the bomb moving almost parallel to the ground.

Certain bridges, ships, buildings, and railroad track embankments were suitable targets for minimum-altitude bombing. It was crucial to study terrain surrounding targets so that aircraft could try to avoid trees, power lines, poles, hills and buildings. Bombing accuracy depended on the skill of the pilots. Missions could fail if bombs missed or bounced off surfaces of targets. This happened often in bridge bombing. Some P-38s were equipped to bomb from relatively high altitudes using a bombsight. In bad weather they were guided to target areas by radar.

Napalm bombs were employed against such targets as fortresses and installations concealed in forests. They started fires of high intensity over a sizable area. Napalm, an incendiary fluid, was contained in droptanks and ignited on impact by a magnesium bomb. The trajectory of the bomb was erratic, and accuracy was difficult to achieve. The technique used was similar to that of minimum-altitude bombing, and there was considerable danger to the fighter-bomber from the exploding tank.

Ground strafing was the most important tactic for fighter-bombers. Machine guns demolished many targets, including locomotives, freight cars, railroad repair equipment, trucks, staff cars, horse-drawn wagons, barges, tugboats, supply dumps, antiaircraft batteries and aircraft on the ground. Fighter-bombers carried more than 6000 rounds of .50 caliber ammunition.

During a strafing attack, pilots tried to avoid approaches too steep or too flat. When it was too steep, the pilot usually opened fire before reaching effective range to avoid flying into the ground. When the approach was too flat, pilots had to concentrate on avoiding obstacles. It was a great help to pilots if the enemy could be surprised. Speed also made the tasks of enemy gunners more difficult.

Fighter-bomber groups put considerable emphasis on interdiction — isolation of a battle area. An important part of interdiction was systematic destruction of railroad centers, bridges, tracks and road traffic. On "armed recc" missions, pilots searched an area for road and rail traffic. They flew at altitudes between 4000 and 6000 feet, just out of range of automatic weapons on the ground. Pilots had multiple goals. Bombs were carried to use on important targets. They also had responsibility for reconnaissance.

As two of the Third Army's corps drove south in August, XIX TAC gave them air support whenever weather allowed operations and XIX TAC was not diverted to other campaigns.

4

The Drive to the Loire

Early in August, Bradley warned Patton that the enemy might launch a counterattack to isolate the Third Army. Patton put several divisions in readiness to counter such a move. At about the same time, Hitler ordered von Kluge to launch precisely the kind of offensive that Bradley had forecast. Five panzer divisions would attempt to break through the right side of the 12th Army Group's line and drive west nineteen miles to capture Avranches. Hitler sent these instructions to von Kluge:

> The enemy is not under any circumstances to be permitted to break out into the open. Army Group B will prepare a counterattack, using all Panzer units, to push through as far as Avranches, cut off the enemy units that have broken through and destroy them. All available Panzer forces are to be withdrawn from their present front sectors, even if there are no divisions to relieve them, and are to be employed for this purpose under the commanding general of the Panzer troops, Eberbach. The outcome of the campaign in France depends upon this counterattack.[1]

In an evaluation of his general officers, Eisenhower once wrote that Bradley had a knack of divining the enemy's intentions. It was probably a tongue-in-cheek comment.

Bradley had excellent sources of intelligence, including French civilians, aerial reconnaissance and prisoners of war. He did not have to rely on intuition. His best source of intelligence about high-level German plans came in a steady stream with the designation "TOP SECRET ULTRA."

Allied air forces and French Resistance fighters had disrupted communications lines between Hitler's and von Kluge's headquarters. Von Kluge received orders from Hitler and sent reports to him by radio. Allied intelligence services intercepted these transmissions, decrypted the messages, and sent their contents to Allied commanders, often within a few hours. This source gave Allied leaders priceless information about German plans, strengths and moves. It was intelligence of the highest grade — timely, reliable and accurate. Other sources of information often provided out-of-date, unreliable material, but not ULTRA. Other sources told of events that happened or were happening. ULTRA revealed German plans for the future. This quality of intelligence provided by ULTRA helped the Allies spring traps on German forces. One of the most important took place in early August near Mortain, a town 19 miles east of Avranches.

Important German radio messages were encrypted by a complex electrical machine called Enigma. It looked like a typewriter. Both senders and recipients had Enigma machines to encrypt and decrypt messages. Germans believed that Enigma's construction and procedures for using it were too complex to be unraveled by enemy intelligence services. They were wrong, and it was a mortal mistake. Polish mathematicians learned how to read Enigma messages in the thirties. When the war started they gave their discoveries to French and British intelligence services.

British intelligence agents had tried to break the Enigma system without success. They immediately recognized the value of the Polish gift. They set up a vast organization to exploit it and safeguard its security. The Germans never learned during the war that the Allies could decrypt Enigma messages.[2] ULTRA gave SHAEF information of tremendous value about the effectiveness of Allied deception campaigns.

Major M. C. Helfers, the officer who handled ULTRA messages at Third Army headquarters, quickly earned Patton's confidence. On August 8 Helfers received a long ULTRA message about a German offensive to capture Avranches. Helfers took the message and a map to Patton's trailer. As a result of this briefing, Patton ordered two divisions to prepare to block the German thrust. Patton told Helfers to give him a briefing early each morning on ULTRA information received in the past twenty-four hours. He ordered Helfers to come to him or his chief of staff immediately whenever he received information requiring prompt action.

As a former cavalryman, Patton respected intelligence gathering. Helfers recorded that, "General Patton fully appreciated the value of ULTRA, but he did not lose all perspective concerning it as did General Hodges and his staff at First Army and as did General Bradley and his staff at Twelfth U.S. Army Group."[3] This comment of Helfer's refers to an opinion widespread among intelligence analysts familiar with ULTRA that some commanders placed too much reliance on it. When Germans cloaked operations in radio silence, ULTRA could not provide much information about them.

ULTRA kept Eisenhower, Montgomery and Bradley well informed about Hitler's orders to capture Avranches. Von Kluge's messages showed his forebodings about the operation. He knew it was madness to mass tanks in daylight; they would be blasted out of action by fighter-bombers, artillery, anti-tank weapons and Allied armor. He warned Hitler: "…the execution of this order means the collapse of the whole Normandy front."[4]

Eisenhower decided to keep part of the Third Army driving eastward. He and Bradley perceived an opportunity to encircle the German counterattack force and annihilate it. Eisenhower told Patton that the Third Army could be supplied by air if it was cut off. Encirclement was also on Hitler's mind. The Third Army's drive offered an opportunity to encircle and destroy it. Hitler decided that this goal made the risks worth taking, despite von Kluge's misgivings.

Bradley was amazed at the risks the Germans were taking. So were the German commanders, but Hitler made decisions at his headquarters—far from Normandy. On July 20 Hitler had survived an attempted assassination by German army officers. The experience deepened his distrust of his commanders, including von Kluge. They, in turn, feared that any opposition to Hitler's orders would be construed by him as treason. The Gestapo was rounding up suspected conspirators. Some of them were brutally tortured and then executed. Others, including Rommel, were forced to commit suicide.

Three panzer divisions, with nearly 190 tanks, opened the counteroffensive shortly after midnight on August 7. Elements of the U.S. 3rd Armored and 30th Infantry Divisions were in the path of the German drive. Hitler hoped for surprise, but Bradley expected the enemy offensive and was waiting to crush it. Artillery fire pounded German armor. When the skies cleared, German tank crews knew they would be attacked by fighter-bombers.

A key objective for German forces was Mortain. The 2nd SS Panzer Division overran the town, but elements of the 30th Division held high ground in the area. From these heights they directed artillery fire on enemy troops.

RAF and Ninth Air Force fighter-bombers attacked targets around Mortain throughout the day. Only 30 tanks survived the carnage. IX TAC flew 429 sorties to the Mortain region, and XIX TAC sent P-51 groups to the battle.[5]

Leigh-Mallory reported that 19 squadrons of Typhoons (RAF fighter-bombers) flew 59 missions, comprising 458 sorties against the panzer divisions near Mortain. They fired more than 2000 rockets and dropped 80 tons of bombs. AEAF reports claimed that the RAF destroyed 83 tanks and "probably destroyed" 29 more.[6]

The fate of the German offensive was decided in the first twenty-four hours. Superb intelligence prevented surprise. Clear weather aided air attacks and artillery fire. Fierce resistance by American soldiers stopped German panzer forces. Eisenhower, Montgomery, and Bradley took a bold gamble by letting the Third Army continue its drive to the east. First Army and British forces to the north, and the Third Army to the south, threatened to encircle the panzer army.

On August 7, surrounded elements of the 30th Division refused a German demand to surrender. AAF C-47 transports and liaison aircraft dropped food , ammunition and medical supplies to the Americans on August 9–10. In battles around Mortain, the 30th Infantry Division "fought as hard as any unit was to fight in the European Theater," a U.S. Army history records.

This same history concluded that, "Chance had played an important role in the American reaction."[7] The role of ULTRA was not disclosed until a quarter century after war's end. Chance did not put American divisions in the right places to put devastating artillery fire on German troops. It was Allied intelligence, not chance, that put the Ninth Air Force and the RAF's 2nd Tactical Air Force on alert to strike at German armor.

On August 11 von Kluge convinced Hitler that the offensive had no chance to capture Avranches. He received Hitler's grudging permission to withdraw forces around Mortain to deal with the threat the Third Army posed to his southern flank. German commanders reported to von Kluge that, "The attack has been brought to a complete standstill by unusually strong fighter-bomber activities."[8]

On August 7 XIX TAC increased in size to nine groups of fighter-bombers. The distances separating Third Army columns meant that XIX TAC's aircraft spent large amounts of time flying to and from battle areas, and less time fighting. It needed greater strength to adapt to this problem. Furthermore, Patton had given XIX TAC important reconnaissance missions which required more groups. Close air support for the Third Army became more difficult to provide as Patton's columns raced in different directions. XIX TAC was tied to its airfields. Aviation engineers performed crucial work constructing airfields closer to the fronts.

The Third Army's drive eastward to the Seine River started on August 3 when Bradley instructed Patton to clear the area west of Mayenne as far south as the Loire. Patton claimed to be unconcerned about having an open right flank. "If I had worried about flanks," he wrote, "I could never have fought the war. Also I was convinced that our Air Service could locate any groups of enemy large enough to be a serious threat, and then I could always pull something out of the hat to drive them back while the Air Force in the meantime delayed their advance."[9]

4. The Drive to the Loire

Engineers constructing an airfield in France (courtesy of NARA).

A U.S. Army history explains that this comment should not be taken at face value: "Contrary to the Patton legend he appreciated the possibility that German troops might make sorties against Third Army's right in the 'no man's land' between the Loire and Loir."[10] In addition to his confidence in his air support, Patton had help from the French Resistance to keep German troops off balance. He also had accurate intelligence about German difficulties. Allied air forces had blocked most of the bridges on the Loire. Patton knew that an Allied invasion of southern France, scheduled for August 15, would occupy the attention of German forces south of the Loire. He also knew that their objective was to retreat to Germany to escape capture. They were not planning to attack the Third Army.

To help guard the Third Army against attacks on its flank, however unlikely, XIX TAC executed extensive reconnaissance in the Loire region. Roads, railway lines, and marshalling yards in the area were kept under surveillance. When Allied reconnaissance pilots spotted German forces they called on XIX TAC's fighter-bombers to attack them. German movements were also delayed by Resistance actions.

In early August, the Third Army's XX Corps, commanded by Major

General Walton H. Walker, had paused near Avranches until it became clear that the German counteroffensive had failed to penetrate the 12th Army Group's line.

Walker matched Patton in aggressiveness and boldness. Born in Texas in 1889, Walker, like Patton attended the Virginia Military Institute. Like Patton, he also transferred to the U.S. Military Academy at West Point. He served in the Mexican expedition and fought in France in World War I. In World War II, Walker commanded, in succession, the 3rd Armored Division, the IV Armored Corps, and XX Corps.[11]

On August 7 Patton ordered Walker to send one of the 5th Infantry Division's regiments to seize Angers, an important city near the Loire estuary. Columns of 5th Division vehicles stretched for miles. The 5th Division captured an intact railroad bridge over the Loir (a tributary of the Loire), which gave access to the city. 5th Division troops entered Angers on August 11 and bagged 2000 prisoners.[12]

Nantes, a port at the mouth of the Loire, was held by a strong German garrison with instructions from Hitler to fight "to the last man and the last cartridge," and to destroy the port's installations before the last shot was fired. SHAEF decided not to assault Nantes but to contain its garrison with minimal forces, preferably French Résistants. Walker sent a battalion to block any sorties the Germans might attempt.

When the U.S. Seventh Army invaded southern France, XXIX TAC was formed to support it. XIX TAC was trimmed to five fighter-bomber groups (the 354th, 358th, 362nd, 405th and 406th Groups, and the 10th photo reconnaissance group).

XIX TAC continued to guard the Third Army's open flank, in addition to flying missions in support of VIII Corps at Brest. It dispatched tactical, photographic and armed reconnaissance units to check on German moves in the Loire area. The 373rd Fighter Group destroyed 15 freight cars near Blois on August 9. Two days later the 405th Fighter Group bombed a train loaded with 60 tanks.

Weyland later described a conversation with Patton about the Loire flank: "It was wide open about 400 or 500 miles. Old Georgie [Patton] says, 'Aw, to hell with it. You take care of that.' There wasn't very much down south, but they did start up and try to move up. Well, first of all, we decided that we wouldn't let them get back to Germany and we cut rail lines and so on. Then they started moving toward our flanks. So we'd clobber them and they never got there."[13]

On August 19 fighter-bomber pilots reported fires and explosions in Paris and its environs. The next day the roads east of Paris were clogged with German trucks and wagons, many drawn by animals. Downstream

In a group of Third Army officers, Brig. Gen. Otto Weyland stands behind Patton (center), on the right, and Maj. Gen. Walton Walker is front right in the photograph (courtesy of NARA).

from Paris, German forces crossed the Seine in many places using a variety of vessels.

During the Third Army's drive to the Loire, XIX TAC sent armed reconnaissance airplanes east of Paris, and far south of the Loire. A report of the 362nd Fighter Group gives a picture of typical fighter-bomber missions:

> "Four 500-pound bombs dropped on enemy guns; 8 fragmentation clusters and two 500-pound bombs dropped on a marshaling yard; 48 box cars and a locomotive destroyed; miscellaneous motor vehicles strafed; 15 freight cars loaded with 155 mm guns strafed and damaged; 26 bombs dropped on 7 Tiger tanks."[14]

XIX TAC never caught up with the Third Army in August. General Weyland made it a practice to fly to Third Army headquarters each day to confer with Patton.

Army headquarters moved with its forward units to shorten its communication lines, but groups could not change airfields so readily. On one occasion XIX TAC moved forward with the Third Army in advance of its landlines, but because of a lack of sufficient communications, the subsequent operations were unsatisfactory. Weyland vowed to avoid this in future.

In order to maintain liaison with the Third Army during rapid advances, XIX TAC organized a small detachment of operations and signals personnel to keep within radio range of ground forces while the main headquarters remained behind.

On August 17 the Third Army notified XIX TAC that Chateaudun was clear of Germans. Immediate steps were taken to transfer XIX TAC groups to an excellent airfield there. Because of the speed of the Third Army's advance, the Germans did not have time to demolish the airfield.

Third Army units advanced in different directions in August, with distances between them as much as 350 miles. These separations created serious communication, control, supply and air support problems. Patton wrote to his wife: "This Army covers so much ground that I have to fly in Cubs most places. I don't like it. I feel like a clay pigeon...."[15]

XV Corps drove east, then veered north toward Argentan. XX Corps secured Angers, contained Nantes, then moved toward Chartres. XII Corps drove southeast, with Orléans its objective. VIII Corps (it became part of the Ninth Army in August) cleared Brittany and prepared to assault Brest. Each corps had its own supply and communications lines which had to be protected. Patton asked Weyland to assume responsibility for a large part of this job, in addition to its missions to provide close air support for the Third Army, interdiction, flank security, reconnaissance, bomber escort, air defense, etc.

Reconnaissance gave commanders vital intelligence about enemy forces—their composition, positions, movements, and probable intentions. In the confusion surrounding Third Army operations in August, air reconnaissance often gave commanders information they needed about the locations of their own units. It provided checks on information gleaned from other sources. Reconnaissance planes often executed missions to support the security of ULTRA. If ULTRA warned about an enemy column moving in a certain area, Allied forces would not respond to this information immediately. They sent out reconnaissance aircraft to "discover" the enemy force. This would lead the German commander to believe his force was spotted by Allied aircraft and not betrayed by some security lapse in his communication network.[16]

Tactical reconnaissance [TAC/R] was performed by F-6 [converted P-51] aircraft operating in pairs. The most experienced of the two pilots navigated and searched for targets. The other pilot searched for flak installations and enemy fighters. They usually flew at altitudes between 3500 and 6000 feet so that they could identify objects on the ground. Sustained flight under 3500 feet was impractical because of intense flak and small arms fire.

TAC/R pilots searched areas along the Third Army's fronts to a depth of approximately 100 miles. An area of about 650 square miles could be covered in about one hour by a pair of reconnaissance planes. Route reconnaissance missions checked rail and road lines to a depth of 200 miles behind enemy lines to find targets for interdiction. TAC/R pilots also adjusted artillery fire for long-range guns. They relied principally on visual observations, but their aircraft were also equipped with cameras. They executed photographic reconnaissance in areas where flak was especially heavy. If a situation demanded urgent action they reported it by radio. TAC/R aircraft carried less camera equipment than a photo reconnaissance plane. Having armor and armament, it often operated at low and medium altitudes.

Photographic reconnaissance was the primary responsibility of squadrons flying F-5 [converted P-38] aircraft. These planes were unarmed; they depended on altitude, speed and evasive maneuvers to avoid air and ground attacks. They flew as high as 35,000 feet, but their more common altitude was about 20,000 feet. Photographic reconnaissance could cover an entire battle area for several miles behind the front. Ground commanders could never get enough good photographs about what was ahead of them. F-6s took detailed pictures of key targets such as bridges, marshalling yards, gun positions, enemy headquarters and important road junctions. They photographed targets both before and after attacks. Every day, weather permitting, they provided a continuous stream of information to help commanders judge the enemy's situation.

Ninth Air Force headquarters directed reconnaissance photography and interpretation. Reconnaissance groups were composed of a photographic reconnaissance squadron, two tactical reconnaissance squadrons, one photographic technical unit and a photographic interpretation unit.

The 10th Photographic Reconnaissance Group bore the primary responsibility for Ninth Air Force photographic missions. It had 34 F-5s, 45 F-6s, 17 F-3s (converted A-20 attack bombers), and six liaison aircraft. Its motto was: "We make pictures that even Generals can interpret."[17]

On a typical day the Group flew 20 area search missions, four road and railroad search missions, four artillery adjustment missions and two map-making missions.

On night photographic missions, F-3 aircraft carried a pilot, navigator and observer/gunner. To illuminate ground areas they dropped flash bombs or operated lights powered by the aircraft's engines. Night photography was inefficient throughout the war.[18]

Bomb damage photographs told commanders when a target needed more attention. ORS units used them to evaluate bombing results.

Ninth Air Force headquarters directed reconnaissance photography. Each TAC had a reconnaissance staff to coordinate reconnaissance activities within the command.

The A-20 attack bomber was initially assigned to support ground troops. It also executed reconnaissance missions. It had speed and maneuverability that permitted it to operate at low altitudes. Flak was so prevalent, however, that A-20s had to fly at altitudes between 8000 and 14,000 feet.[19]

The Third Army's rapid drives in August made tactical reconnaissance much more important than photographic reconnaissance. Photographs were often unnecessary when they arrived at Third Army headquarters because its units had already overrun the ground in the photographs. XIX TAC flew 432 TAC/R missions in August, compared with 81 photographic reconnaissance missions. TAC/R missions were planned by XIX TAC headquarters staff. Tactical areas were subdivided into areas or routes of a size that could be searched during a single mission.[20]

Information obtained during TAC/R missions that needed urgent attention was transmitted by the pilot over VHF radio to the corps or division that needed it.

XIX TAC examined all requests from Third Army units for TAC/R and photographic reconnaissance missions. Photographs were "interpreted," that is, examined closely by the 20th Photo Intelligence Detachment. Ninth Air Force photographic processing units could handle approximately 15,000 prints daily and occasionally more than 44,000 prints in a single day. First-priority prints were produced within six hours and delivered to Third Army units.

"Armed recce" was the term used to designate missions of fighter-bombers, bombed up and loaded with ammunition, assigned to search specific areas visually. They were not trained especially for reconnaissance, nor were they as proficient at it as TAC/R pilots. TAC/R pilots often cooperated with fighter-bomber pilots by guiding them to targets. The abilities of fighter-bomber pilots to carry out reconnaissance missions varied widely. These missions required a high level of navigation and target-spotting skills. It was not enough to identify a target; someone had to be told precisely where it was located using map coordinates.

A XIX TAC intelligence officer remembered a radio report by a fighter-bomber pilot of a train beneath him. Not until he was later interviewed by the intelligence officer was it learned that the train was an ammunition train and that it was headed away from the front rather than toward it.

In mid–August, as the Third Army prepared to cross the Loing River southeast of Paris, the 10th Group received a request to photograph all bridges across this river for a distance of sixty miles. The mission was flown and the Third Army received a report of the pilot's visual observations on the morning of the flight. Photographs were sent to the Third Army in the afternoon and gave considerable help in planning the river-crossing operations.

Despite thick cloud cover on August 23, TAC/R aircraft of the 10th Group led fighter-bombers to German troops retreating east of Paris. They destroyed 114 motor vehicles, 63 horse-drawn wagons, and four tanks.

On August 26, the 10th Photo Reconnaissance Group moved to Châteaudun. This was closer to the front, but F-6 Mustangs on artillery-spotting missions still had to land at Rennes to refuel either before or after missions. Many times, planes had to fly for an hour before reaching their target area. They could remain there for only twenty to thirty minutes.[21]

Liaison aircraft performed vital chores for 10th Group by delivering important photographic prints to Third Army units that needed them quickly. These small airplanes, often called "puddle-jumpers," executed a wide range of missions for both air and ground forces. Their slow speeds at low altitudes made them useful for close examination of areas that were difficult for fighter-bombers or reconnaissance aircraft to check out. Like engineers, communications specialists, and ordnance experts liaison aircraft units were an essential part of the Ninth Air Force.

5

Ninth Air Force Engineers, Liaison Operations, Interdiction and Communications

During its operations in support of OVERLORD, the Ninth Air Force operated over a vast area. Mustangs using droptanks could strike targets 600 miles from their bases. Other Ninth Air Force aircraft — B-26 medium bombers, A-20 light bombers, P-47s, P-38s — also had substantial ranges. The ability to hit targets scattered over a large area is a tremendous advantage of air forces, but it is somewhat limited by their dependence on airdromes. A large number of highly skilled personnel and a large amount of complex equipment are employed to keep aircraft flying on combat operations.

In the months before D-Day, General Brereton warned that Ninth Air Force units had to be able to move from one base to another quickly. To be effective, a tactical air force has to remain close to the armies it supports. It has to develop procedures for moving often, smoothly, and with minimal interruption in operations.

XIX TAC improvised to cope with conditions it faced in France. It developed a system by which fighter-bombers could refuel at airfields closer to the front. This increased their time over target areas. During August and September, eight XIX TAC groups moved twice, and one moved three times. They used the few transport aircraft available, civilian vehicles and those abandoned by the Germans. To minimize disruption during moves, fighter-bomber groups moved in echelons, one remaining in place while the other moved to the new base. XIX TAC's advanced headquarters moved five times in August to remain near Patton's headquarters.

Airmen never knew what conditions they would find at their next

Engineers laying Square Mesh Track (courtesy of NARA).

base. Often they lived in tents or shanties. Some found quarters in permanent buildings. Weather usually treated them kindly in August and September but worsened in October. Some ground personnel had worked in miserable weather conditions in the U.K. in the winter of 1943–44. This experience prepared them to cope with winter weather on the Continent in 1944–45, the worst in many decades.

In the planning stages of OVERLORD it was foreseen that tactical air groups would have to operate from crude runways and airfields, some of them recently carved out of pastures and meadows. Engineers used Square Mesh Track [SMT] in the first months of the invasion for runway surfaces. It was made of wire joined in 3-inch squares, and could be transported in rolls. It did not increase the bearing capacity of the soil. The major drawback of SMT was dust. It did not prevent clouds of corrosive sand that propeller backwash blew onto men and equipment. Hay was put under SMT, and shrimp nets were laid under it at some airfields. Water sprinklers dampened runways, but little oil was available for this purpose. Serious dust problems developed in August, and a different surface material was needed. Engineers turned to Prefabricated Hession Surfacing [PHS]. It was burlap, impregnated with asphalt, and delivered in rolls. Laid in

Engineers laying Prefabricated Hessian Surfacing (courtesy of USAFHRA).

double thickness, its seams sealed with asphaltic cement, it provided a dust-free surface, but it had no supporting value in itself. It tended to break down in areas where aircraft landed. Most of XIX TAC's groups flew P-47s. Their weight, when loaded with bombs and ammunition, damaged runways; much effort had to go into maintenance.[1]

From his experience in the Pacific and North African theaters, Brereton learned that an air force needed engineers. He convinced the War Department to create IX Engineer Command in early 1944. It had 17,000 men assigned to four regiments, plus three airborne battalions. In August, IX Engineer Command was organized into two brigades, one for each tactical air command. Some of the men recruited for engineer service with the Ninth Air Force had worked on airfield construction in the U.K. They brushed up on infantry tactics and skills, and learned how to handle mines, unexploded bombs and booby traps.

One of the greatest challenges for engineers was to select airfield sites that would be needed in the future. They hated to put effort and materials into an airfield that would not be used because the front had moved too far away before the airfield could be used for combat operations.

Soft spots in the French soil, undetected by engineer reconnaissance teams, caused major construction problems. They were excavated and refilled with gravel, stones, and rubble from towns that had been bombarded.

In winter, a stronger surface material, Pierced Steel Plank [PSP], was used for runways when available. It was transported in heavy, rectangular sheets. Because of transportation shortages, it was usually reserved for airfields intended for medium bombers.

Shortages of transportation handicapped engineers as it did most Allied units in the ETO. Engineers were scroungers; they developed unorthodox ways to acquire materials. They made heavy use of civilian labor, construction equipment and materials. Many bridges in France were inoperable. Engineers often set up ferries to help move supplies across rivers.

The speed of the Third Army's advances produced many benefits, one of which helped engineers. They found that Germans had often not had time to demolish runways and buildings at airfields they abandoned. IX Engineer Command put these facilities into service quickly.

Airfield construction used vast amounts of material, much of which had to be carried in trucks. They carried dry material to fill soft spots in runways, which became prevalent during rainstorms in early September.

The first AAF airfields in Brittany were completed in nine days. At Rennes, an airfield with concrete runways was rehabilitated in four days. By August 20, four XIX TAC fighter-bomber groups used airfields south of Avranches.

The 832 Aviation Engineer Battalion moved to a major airfield at Rennes on August 11 to repair bomb and demolition damage. Two hundred French civilians worked with the engineers. At an airfield near Chartres, the 832nd lengthened a runway with PSP.[2] With work at Rennes nearly completed by September 3, the battalion moved 175 miles eastward to Châteaudun. IX Engineer Command worked on airfields in the Le Mans area soon after the Third Army captured them, but the troops' rapid Advance meant the airfields were too far from the front before they were completed. This also happened with construction projects near Chartres. These efforts were not entirely wasted, for the airfields were used by transports to deliver supplies. By August 25, 31 airfields had been completed in France. Sixty-one more were begun in September when a serious need for supply and evacuation airfields developed.[3]

When Paris was liberated in late August, the Ninth Air Force used transport aircraft to fly supplies to the city's civilian population. IX Engineer Command put some Paris airfields into operation in a few days. The commander of an engineer regiment was killed by gunfire while searching for sites for airfields near Paris.

High morale, dedication and skill helped engineers achieve their goals, in spite of long hours of dangerous, back-breaking labor. They knew their work was important; they could see its impact when fighter-bombers began operating from runways they had just completed. Engineers often came under sniper fire. Mines, unexploded shells and booby traps had to be cleared.

Germans fought hard to defend Chartres. It was a regrouping point for their forces. After runways were cleared of unexploded bombs on August 26, airfields near Chartres were used by transport aircraft to bring supplies to Paris and the Third Army, and to evacuate wounded personnel.

Shortages of ammunition and gasoline became so critical in September that heavy bombers were assigned to haul supplies. Engineers had to rehabilitate some airfields with concrete runways to handle B-17s and B-24s. These heavily loaded aircraft damaged runways. This increased the work load of airfield maintenance personnel. B-24s were too much for even six inches of concrete on runways of an airfield near St. Dizier.

Flexibility of organization and ingenuity became hallmarks of aviation engineers. To acquire asphalt, they helped local manufacturers resume operations.[4] In the first two weeks of September, engineers renovated eight airfields in the Paris region.

An Army Air Forces history summarizes aviation engineer achievements in France: "During the dash from Normandy to the German frontier, IX Engineer Command put into operational condition a total of sixty airfields, in spite of immense difficulties. Some units had to move as much as 200 miles from one job to another, and as communications lines lengthened and transportation facilities thinned out, the problem of supplies became ever more acute."[5]

When Allied armies advanced east of Paris, a number of air bases came into their possession. These were usually mined, but the Germans often failed to detonate the explosives.

With few exceptions, airfields formerly used by Germans had hard-surfaced runways that could be repaired quickly. Engineers had bomb disposal squads to deal with the large number of unexploded bombs found on almost every captured airfield. An airfield at Dreux with two concrete runways was made operational after they were extended with PSP.[6]

Original plans provided for construction of airfields at virgin sites around Chartres. The speed of the Third Army made these plans impractical. Like those near Le Mans, they would have been too far from front lines before they were completed. On August 29, 400 transports landed at an airfield near Paris loaded with food for Parisians.

Engineer detachments entered Reims on September 3. Transport aircraft began to land on airfields in the area with gasoline for the Third Army.

In September, IX Engineer Command received a multitude of assignments. Allied armies needed more supplies than the staggering transportation systems could bring them. The demand for supply and evacuation airfields accelerated. Some Third Army depots refused to give gasoline to engineer units. It was difficult to find enough trucks or railroad cars to carry airfield surfacing materials.

The 2nd Engineer Brigade started work on airfields east of Paris on September 1. Intended for medium bombers, these airfields had to be used by heavy bombers loaded with gasoline. On September 7 the 2nd Brigade started to rehabilitate an airfield at St. Dizier, more than a hundred miles east of Paris. Soon, XIX TAC fighters operated from this airfield.

PHS was used whenever possible. It was the least bulky of available surfacing materials, easier to transport, could be laid rapidly, reduced dust problems, and provided a waterproof cover for runways. Each roll of PHS provided a 300-foot strip. Tearing happened when aircraft had to turn sharply. SMT was often used at places where aircraft were most likely to turn. During winter months PHS was impractical; it was difficult to lay on wet surfaces.

The capture of airfields with concrete runways capable of rehabilitation allowed engineers to build up stocks of PSP. This was fortunate because it became available for fighter-bomber groups in the fall and winter months when weather conditions made use of other runway surface materials impractical.

Small, light, liaison airplanes supported both air and ground forces in hundreds of valuable ways. They helped artillery crews adjust shell fire, performed low-level reconnaissance, transported critical personnel, equipment and materials, including wounded stretcher cases, checked

Characteristics	L-4	L-5
Takeoff Distance	737 feet	633 feet
Landing Distance	605 feet	643 feet
Maximum Speed	87 mph	128 mph
Range	260 miles	450 miles
Landing Speed	38 mph	50 mph

Table 4. Liaison Aircraft

camouflage and march discipline of Allied forces, photographed enemy positions, and directed fighter-bombers to targets. They provided regular courier services. Reconnaissance groups used them to deliver photographic prints to front-line units. Engineers used them to find sites for airfields. They delivered mail. Commanders wished they had twice as many.

The Piper L-4 Grasshopper was derived from the Piper Cub, a popular civilian airplane. It had room for a pilot and passenger. A great many Grasshoppers were produced, and they carried out a wide range of tasks in every Allied theater of war. The L-5 Stinson Sentinel, produced by Vultee Aircraft Corporation, carried a pilot and passenger. It could be adapted to carry wounded soldiers.

Liaison aircraft could perform some reconnaissance missions better than fighter-bombers. Their slow speeds, a passenger who could act as an observer, and maneuverability helped them search the ground from low altitudes. They could land and take off from short sod runways. General Eisenhower often flew in liaison airplanes, as did many other commanders. He complained to the War Department that the L-4 and L-5 were too slow at takeoff, and unable to descend fast enough for reasonable safety when attacked. The AAF reacted by giving the L-5 controllable-pitch propellers.

Liaison "puddlejumpers" gave Patton a means to visit Third Army units hundreds of miles apart. He often used a liaison airplane to visit Eisenhower and Bradley. With many roads, railroads, and bridges destroyed, liaison aircraft became especially valuable.

During the Battle of France, the C-47 was used by many high-ranking officers for their personal transportation. The AAF assigned C-47s to Patton and Bradley for their exclusive use.

The 14th Liaison Squadron supported the Third Army. To facilitate its many changes of base, it developed a leap-frog procedure whereby one echelon maintained operations while another moved to a new base. Liaison aircraft did not need elaborate airfields, but some engineer equipment was necessary to smooth runways. Otherwise, gullies caused crashes and strut breakdowns. Each time the squadron moved, it had to request transportation from the Third Army. Improvised equipment helped the squadron make its moves. It had five large captured trucks, six trailers and four small cars. One trailer carried water, another aircraft oil. One of the cars was fitted for use as a communications center. The 14th Squadron flew 2,084 missions in August.[7] It made nine moves, over a distance of 382 miles. One of the squadron's greatest problems was the lack of special gasoline needed by liaison airplanes. The use of improper gasoline caused a large number of burnt-out intake valves in engines. Navigation and flak also caused trouble. Pilots had to use Michelin road maps to navigate. Flying at tree-top level, they were vulnerable to ground fire and many were hit.

On August 12 Patton asked engineers to open a rail line to Le Mans by August 15. A U.S. Army history records that this request "meant that a railroad 135 miles long, with seven bridges down, three railroad yards badly bombed, track damaged in many places and few, if any, watering and coaling facilities available, had to be reconstructed in seventy-five hours. Normally the job would have taken months."[8]

A rush reconnaissance by air selected lines which could be repaired in the shortest time. Engineers decided to open a single-track line east from Pontaubault to St. Hilaire-du-Harcouet, then southeast to Mayenne, then to connect with a double-track line at Le Mans. Five bridges would have to be restored to service. Elements of eleven engineer regiments worked on the line. Patton's deadline was satisfied when a most difficult restoration of a bridge at St. Hilaire was completed. A train loaded with gasoline arrived in Le Mans two days later.

During the last week of August, elements of three provisional engineer groups, each with an experienced general service regiment as a nucleus, worked on rail lines between Pontaubault and the Seine. After Paris was liberated, engineers opened a line to Versailles.

Throughout the summer of 1944, the Ninth Air Force executed an interdiction campaign in support of U.S. armies. Medium bombers of the Ninth Air Force and heavy bombers of the Eighth Air Force attacked bridges on the Loire. IX Bomber Command put six of them out of service. This campaign made it difficult for German troops south of the Loire to threaten the Third Army's right flank or retreat to Germany.

Ninth Air Force medium and fighter-bombers often hit railroad marshalling yards as part of the interdiction program. Fighter-bombers also bombed tracks. Quesada held unrealistic hopes for track-cutting. He expected that Germans would have great difficulty repairing track cuts in the countryside, where labor was not plentiful. This was true, but the complexity of the French railroad network made it likely that the Germans could find an alternate route to bypass a blocked line. Another drawback was the difficulty of monitoring track cuts in bad weather. AAF operations analysts later concluded that track-cutting programs rarely achieved their principal objectives.[9]

All air campaigns must be adjusted to fit changing circumstances. Interdiction had to be coordinated closely with the progress of Allied armies. When the Third Army raced across France in August, Ninth Air Force planners had to decide whether destruction of transportation targets

Bombed bridge at Rouen (courtesy of USAFHRA).

would hurt American forces more than the enemy. The Third Army's mobility was superior to that of the enemy. Patton knew he could move forces rapidly, provided that his troops were not delayed too often by demolished bridges. German forces relied heavily on animals to pull their wagons and equipment. Many German soldiers rode on bicycles or walked. American soldiers often rode in trucks, jeeps, and armored vehicles.

Toward the end of August, constricted Allied supply lines created a logistics crisis. No major ports had been captured in usable condition. Most Allied supplies came through Cherbourg or over Normandy beaches, and from there by truck over a chaotic road system to the front lines. Much of this devastation had been wrought before the invasion of France. Allied heavy bombers had bombed railroad centers of France and Belgium for months prior to D-Day. This campaign devastated towns around railroad hubs. Demolished railroads had to be repaired by the Allies to supply their forces and the civilian economy. A report issued by XIX TAC in August recommended that, "Air plans should be coordinated with Ground Force Engineers in order to assist the engineers in preparing for rapid repair of rail lines, bridges, and road nets."[10]

The French had complained endlessly about Allied bombing. The Resistance claimed that sabotage was a far more efficient way of disrupting transportation systems. This idea gained few supporters at SHAEF, although Spaatz and other AAF commanders had protested against extensive bombing of rail centers. Air Marshals Harris and Leigh-Mallory favored the assault on French railroads, and they convinced Eisenhower to order it.

Effective interdiction was executed against road traffic. It forced the Germans to move in darkness. Bombing roads themselves was, however, ineffective. Bomb craters were quickly filled, often with rubble from nearby homes. Small bridges on secondary roads could usually be bypassed. The AAF's faith in interdiction, though challenged, remained strong. On August 14, IX Bomber Command received orders from General Vandenberg (who replaced Brereton) clarifying its objectives for the immediate future: "In an overall general priority, communications [interdiction] targets rank first, fuel dumps second and ammunition dumps third.... If rapid repair of a high priority bridge indicates its critical need by the enemy, subsequent attacks will be in such weight as to insure its complete destruction rather than cutting of only one or two spans. High priority targets attacked unsuccessfully will be re-scheduled immediately." Responding to concerns about destruction of French historic buildings, Vandenberg ordered that, "No targets will be attacked in the cities of Rheims and Chartres."[11]

As the Third Army gained ground rapidly in August, its communications units faced enormous problems. It was impossible to maintain telephone and telegraph lines to connect forces moving so rapidly in different directions. Radio became invaluable, but shortages of equipment and trained personnel limited its use. It became necessary to put more stations than was desirable on a single network. All signals battalions were short of wire and other communications gear, and they lacked trucks to bring supplies from the beaches. Wire crews labored to install at least one circuit between Third Army headquarters and each corps. Couriers carried important messages in jeeps and light aircraft through regions full of disorder, devastation and hazards. Commanders often directed their units without clear, current orders from higher authority.

With its strong cavalry traditions, Third Army personnel coped well with disruption and lack of direction. Patton expected subordinates to make decisions and initiate actions without waiting for specific instructions and hand-holding from superior officers.[12]

It was difficult to supply fast-moving armored forces. General Wood, commander of the 4th Armored Division, described the operations of his supply vehicles: "The trucks were like a band of stage coaches making a run through Indian country."[13]

A Third Army signal officer remembered the early days of the drive across France: "Wire supplies became critical, and only through the superhuman efforts of our Signal supply personnel could we obtain enough to continue the advance. We were using it faster than it could be brought forward. We were advised to recover our old wire before moving on, but had neither the time nor the personnel to do it."[14]

Communications between tanks and aircraft operated smoothly. Airmen assigned to tank columns communicated with pilots using VHF radios and language that both fully understood, so that there was little chance of confusion or misunderstanding. Air liaison officers would rarely ask pilots to attack targets that were not suitable for air attacks.

In August, Third Army headquarters moved eight times. Signal battalions kept moving radio relay systems from hill to hill to keep Patton's staff in touch with other Allied forces.

When Third Army headquarters moved, General Patton would pick a location for the next command post. The signals unit would then extend the wire axis toward that point. An advance group, always in radio communication with the rear, went forward to select the actual site as soon as it was captured. When wire communications were established, the forward echelon of the Third Army would move in and the process would be repeated.[15]

XIX TAC had enormous communications difficulties. It had to communicate with both air and ground units scattered over a large area. Air-ground communications were troubled by crowded channels, unreliable reception and poor radio discipline of pilots and others sending or receiving messages. Germans contributed to the chaos in the ether by jamming channels and transmitting false reports to Allied pilots.

Communications are the nerve system of an air force. To maintain effective contact between ground and air forces, an air force radio team was attached to each corps and division. Artillery battalions communicated by radio with reconnaissance pilots to adjust fire of long-range guns. When armored combat commands operated separately (as they often did), each had an air-ground communications team.

Reconnaissance groups relied heavily on radio. TAC/R pilots reported targets directly to a fighter control center which then directed fighter-bombers and reconnaissance aircraft to rendezvous points. Much time and effort could be saved, and chances for successful missions improved, when targets spotted by reconnaissance pilots were assigned to fighter-bombers already in the area.[16]

Air and ground forces quickly discovered that one of the best ways to foster effective communications was to have sections that worked together share adjacent quarters. Whenever possible, headquarters of the Third Army and XIX TAC were located near each other. The Ninth Air Force kept its headquarters near that of the 12th Army Group. With ground forces moving rapidly, each air organization in the theater had to be kept informed about what others were doing at any given time. This was essential to avoid waste, confusion, mishaps, and lost opportunities.[17]

After the panzer counteroffensive to take Avranches failed, the Third Army advanced rapidly eastward against weak opposition from German forces in retreat.

6

XV Corps at Argentan

Based on information from ULTRA decrypts and other sources, Eisenhower, Montgomery and Bradley concluded that Allied forces might be able to encircle and capture the German divisions moving eastward from the area around Mortain. Montgomery ordered the First Canadian Army to drive south toward Falaise, where it would be the northern jaw of a trap. Bradley ordered Patton to send part of the Third Army north from Alençon to meet Canadian forces near Argentan, a town 16 miles south of Falaise.

Montgomery did not favor a meeting of the Third Army and the First Canadian Army south of Falaise. He preferred to push the German forces toward the Seine River, pounded by artillery and air power along the way, and surround them there. Nevertheless, he allowed Bradley to send the Third Army northward toward Falaise.[1] Patton ordered XV Corps, commanded by Maj. Gen. Wade Haislip, to push toward Argentan. German panzer divisions were occupying positions to keep an escape route open.

XV Corps turned to the north on August 10 reinforced by the 2nd French Armored Division, commanded by Major General Jacques Leclerc.

XIX TAC was alerted to give strong support to XV Corps. It maintained a high rate of operations in August. Squadrons flew three missions each day, and some flew five. They averaged eleven hours and forty-five minutes in the air. One squadron, flying air cover for XV Corps in the Le Mans area, encountered 12 enemy fighters and destroyed seven of them. P-51 pilots of the 363rd Fighter Group scored 12 victories in the Paris area.[2]

On August 11 von Kluge received permission from Hitler to attack XV Corps. ULTRA warned Bradley of the threat.

XV Corps had joined the Third Army early in August. During its first days of operations the 90th Infantry Division captured St. Hilaire-du-Harcouet, 15 miles southeast of Avranches. The 79th Infantry Division cleared the enemy from Fougéres.

After the German counteroffensive ceased to be a serious threat, Patton told Haislip to sweep eastward and not stop to wipe out pockets of

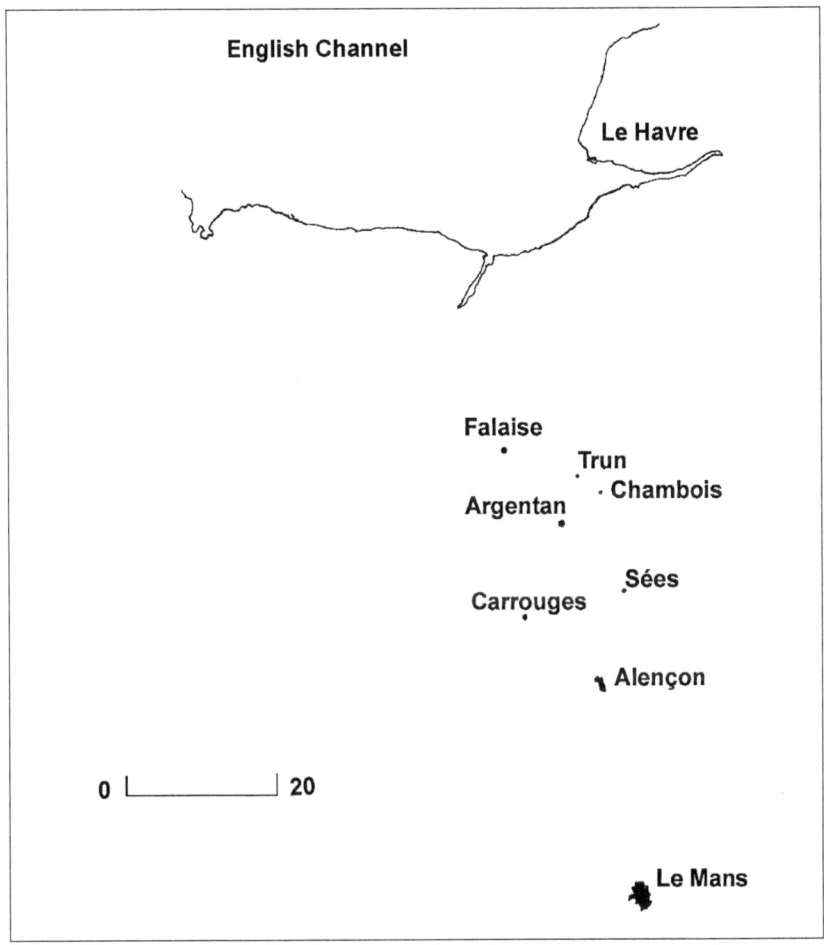

Map 3. XV Corps' Objectives, August 9–12, 1944

resistance. XV Corps's infantry divisions captured bridgeheads across the Mayenne River at Laval and Mayenne, and its 5th Armored Division took Le Mans.

XV Corps advanced toward Argentan with the 2nd French Armored and 90th Infantry Divisions on the left, and the 5th Armored and 79th Infantry Divisions on the right. With two armored and two infantry divisions moving through a region with few good roads, traffic discipline was critical.

Several forests south of Argentan gave the Germans good cover and concealment. Haislip instructed Leclerc to bypass Fôret d'Ecouves. The

French commander did not always comply promptly with orders from Americans. Sometimes he ignored them. Leclerc decided to send one combat command east of the Fôret d'Ecouves, one through it, and a third west of it. The results of these moves were catastrophic. French units on the right trespassed on roads Haislip had assigned to the 5th Armored Division. Road congestion delayed an attack by the 5th Armored for six hours at a crucial time when tough German panzer units were moving into the Argentan area. When the 5th Armored finally attacked, it made little progress.

During its march from the Normandy beaches, the 2nd French Armored Division had met few good German divisions but many French civilians generous with wine, cheers, flowers and kisses. It had developed a certain reckless élan.

The French combat command that marched into the forest met tough opposition, tougher than any the 2nd French Armored Division had encountered in France. The French tanks marched in column. The leading tank was knocked out with one shot. The tank that took its place at the head of the column suffered the same fate. Slowly the French pressed on. Four tanks were knocked out in a hundred yards and casualties were heavy.

Leclerc arrived at the scene of the carnage and urged his men to push ahead. A tank that originally had been tenth became first. Armored infantry moved through the woods using rifles, bayonets and grenades to flush out German infantry and anti-tank crews. German Tiger tanks with 88 mm high-velocity guns continued to pound the French armor. Wounded men abandoned burning tanks and staggered to the rear. Slowly the French pushed the enemy from the forest.[3]

This fight must have increased Bradley's concern about road congestion and the quality of German opposition. In the following days it influenced his decision about closing a trap on the Germans.

Patton wanted XV Corps to take Argentan and then advance toward Falaise, but panzer divisions had set up defensive positions around the town.

On August 12 Haislip ordered Leclerc to take Argentan. It was a necessary preliminary to XV Corps' moves to meet Canadian forces south of Falaise. If successful, this operation would close a pocket that contained large numbers of Germans and vast amounts of equipment. In response to Bradley's concern about moving the Third Army into a sector assigned to the British, Patton ordered Haislip to "push on slowly in the direction of Falaise." It was unusual to find the word "slowly" in a message from Patton, but the situation required caution.

The 2nd French Armored Division entered Argentan on August 13 but could not clear the city. The German commander, General Eberbach, continued to reinforce positions in and around Argentan. On this day, Bradley ordered Patton to stop XV Corps' drive to close the Falaise pocket. Patton sent Haislip the following message: "Elements of your command which may be in the vicinity of FALAISE or to the north of ARGENTAN who are not fighting, should be gradually withdrawn to the ARGENTAN area." Patton recorded his disgust with this order: "It is very regrettable that the XV Corps was ordered to halt, because it could have gone on to Falaise and made contact with the Canadians northwest of that point and definitely and positively closed the escape gap."[4]

Patton made several attempts to contact Bradley to request a change in the order to halt XV Corps. He flew to SHAEF's headquarters where Bradley was visiting Eisenhower. Patton often flew to see Bradley to clarify issues. Bradley refused to change the order.

Canadian and Polish forces met strong German resistance as they moved toward Falaise. Formidable German 88 mm guns took a heavy toll on armor. A Canadian historian wrote: "Such losses would have been deeply regrettable even had they been the price of success. Unfortunately, they were suffered in the course of a tactical reverse which did much to prevent us from seizing a strategic opportunity of the first magnitude."[5] During this period, thousands of German soldiers escaped from the Falaise pocket.

An ULTRA decrypt reported on August 15 that two battle groups of the 2nd SS Panzer Division would reach the Argentan area during the night. This division fought hard to keep the Falaise gap open and allow German soldiers to escape capture.

After XV Corps ended its drive toward Falaise, Bradley told Patton to send a task force east to the Seine. Bradley wanted to secure a bridgehead over this important river to "thwart the enemy's last bright chance for defense of the Seine River line."[6]

Bradley's decision to halt XV Corps at Argentan has provoked much debate. Some military experts believe it allowed a significant number of German soldiers to escape through the Falaise gap. Bradley defended his decision by claiming, among other reasons, that Allied air forces had dropped delayed-action bombs in the Falaise pocket.

A far more important reason for the halt order was the danger that Canadians and Americans could collide if XV Corps continued its advance into a British sector.

Allied air forces did not accept Bradley's excuse. A few delay-action bombs, usually set to explode within a few hours, should not cause the cancellation of a major offensive.

Allied forces did collide during the hectic operations of August, but precautions could have been set up to avoid such mishaps or minimize their effects if they did occur.

During the retreat of German forces from the Falaise pocket, a SHAEF order annoyed Allied airmen. To reduce the likelihood of Allied aircraft hitting friendly forces, the AEAF was ordered to cease attacking targets in the pocket. The AEAF commander complained that over-cautious restrictions on air activity helped the enemy at a time when he was vulnerable to air attacks.[7]

In his postwar book, Bradley explained that he did not have authority to send troops north of the boundary line separating 21 Army Group and 12 Army Group sectors. Only Montgomery could make changes in army group boundaries.[8]

A U.S. Army history explains that in the Allied command structure, "finesse, good manners, and the subtleties of coalition warfare required the responsible commander to make the responsible decision without prompting, and this only Montgomery—or Eisenhower—could have done."[9]

Bradley's concern about unit boundaries was warranted. On August 13 the 80th and 90th Infantry Divisions became badly mixed up during operations south of Argentan.

In his book, Bradley accepted full responsibility for his decision to halt XV Corps at Argentan, but he was critical of the 21 Army Group for slowness in taking Falaise. He remembered that, "a shocked Third Army looked on helplessly as its quarry fled [and] Patton raged at Montgomery's blunder." To Bradley it seemed as if the British were trying to push the Germans out of the pocket instead of trapping them in it.[10]

Eisenhower later wrote an excuse for Montgomery—and implicitly for himself—about the failure to close the gap at Falaise. He explained that the rapid movements of U.S. forces made it impossible for Montgomery "to achieve the hour-by-hour coordination that might have won us a complete battle of annihilation."[11]

After several costly battles and delays, the First Canadian Army approached Falaise. Losses were heavy but armor broke through enemy lines, and infantry established positions a few miles from Falaise. The town was cleared of Germans on August 17.

Elements of nine German infantry and five panzer divisions continued to stream out of the Falaise pocket through a gap six to ten miles wide. Montgomery ordered Polish and Canadian forces to push on toward Trun, a town a few miles east of Falaise. He directed Bradley to take Chambois, a town northeast of Argentan.

Montgomery sent a directive to General Henry D. Crerar, commander of the First Canadian Army: "It is absolutely essential that both armoured divisions of the 2nd Canadian Corps ... close the gap between First Canadian and Third U.S. Army. 1st Polish Armoured Division must thrust on past Trun to Chambois at all costs and as quickly as possible."[12]

Having sent part of XV Corps east to the Seine, Patton organized a provisional corps to take Chambois. It consisted of the 80th Infantry, 90th Infantry and 2nd French Armored Divisions. He sent his chief of staff, Major General Hugh Gaffey, to command it. At this time Bradley made a most unfortunate move. Without notifying Patton, he ordered Major General Leonard Gerow to take command of the provisional corps. Gerow was not familiar with the area or the situation. Gaffey was on the scene in command of the provisional corps. Gerow had to travel through the night in heavy rain to get to corps headquarters near Alençon.[13] Because of the switch from Gaffey to Gerow, the attack was delayed from August 17 to August 18. Every hour's delay allowed hundreds of German soldiers to escape.

With discipline and courage in the midst of chaos and carnage, German troops moved through the Falaise gap in relatively good order. Despite murderous air and artillery attacks, they fought to keep escape routes open. Vehicles clogged roads, and dead animals littered the countryside. Corpses of German soldiers were stacked in piles. A German soldier described one scene: "The crossing of the bridge over the Dives was a particularly ghastly affair. Men, horses, vehicles and other equipment that had been shot-up while making the crossing, had crashed from the bridge into the deep ravine of the Dives and lay there jumbled together in gruesome heaps."[14]

On August 19, Polish and American troops met in Chambois. The Falaise pocket was closed, but German soldiers continued to fight to break out. In battles around Chambois, panzer forces, badly understrength, engaged American and Polish armor to help keep vital escape routes to the Seine open. The 2nd Panzer Division attacked Allied forces and rallied troops struggling to get out of the pocket. A U.S. Army history states: "The major factor deciding the outcome of the breakout operation was the determination and the will to fight of the units inside the pocket."[15]

Until ordered to stop, Allied air forces attacked the retreating German columns. XIX TAC's fighter-bombers damaged 1,000 road and rail carriers, 45 tanks and armored vehicles, and 12 locomotives. They leveled 10 strongpoints. Congestion in the pocket and lack of fuel forced some crews to abandon their tanks. The ratio of abandonment to destruction by air or ground attack was 5:1, but air attacks helped create conditions which forced crews to abandon vehicles. The Ninth Air Force destroyed

84 tanks. On August 13 the 36th Fighter Group discovered a German column in the Argentan area. It destroyed 450 motor transport vehicles. On August 19 XIX TAC destroyed 20 Seine barges and damaged 91 more.[16]

The pounding of German forces by Allied air forces led some observers to suggest that it was not necessary to trap them; they could be wiped out by air attack. It was an unrealistic assumption. German troops had developed a high level of expertise in moving troops and equipment in darkness and under cloud cover. They used camouflage efficiently. In clear daylight they dispersed into woods and dug shelters in ditches and hedgerows. Most soldiers acted as aircraft spotters.

The RAF 2nd Tactical Air Force was active in the battles in the Falaise-Argentan area. Typhoon fighter-bombers flew 2193 sorties against targets in the region. They fired 10,000 rockets and dropped 400 tons of bombs. In these actions pilots claimed destruction of 104 tanks.[17]

Ninth Air Force operations analysts studied 1089 motor vehicles lost by the Germans in the Falaise Pocket. This figure included 90 tanks. Fighter-bombers destroyed 452 of the vehicles in this sample, six of them tanks. Crews abandoned 65 tanks. Most of the damage done by aircraft was caused by machine-gun or cannon fire. Bombs and rockets destroyed relatively few vehicles. Investigators could not always ascertain precisely how a burnt-out tank was destroyed or why a vehicle was abandoned. Road blocks and lack of fuel caused crews to abandon some vehicles.[18]

Major General James M. Gavin, commander of the 82nd Airborne Division, wrote a book about campaigns in the ETO. He found it difficult to understand why the Falaise gap was not closed sooner. "General Bradley should have gone forward at least to Patton's headquarters to discuss the situation with him on August 13," he wrote. "...By removing themselves from the scene of action and at the same time tying Patton's hands, Eisenhower and Bradley allowed at least half of two German armies to escape."[19]

As commander of Allied ground forces, Montgomery bore major responsibility for the failure to close the Falaise pocket sooner. A history of the Battle of the Falaise Gap is critical of Montgomery: "By waffling, by expecting failure in the shallow envelopment, Montgomery virtually assured that result."[20]

Leclerc told Patton on August 15 that "if he were not allowed to advance on Paris, he would resign." Patton was not amused by this insubordination. He recorded in his diary that he informed Leclerc that he "would not have division commanders tell me where they could fight.... We parted friends."[21]

Leclerc was in a somewhat ambiguous position. His division was a part of the Third Army but his commander-in-chief was de Gaulle, who had told him that it was top priority for the 2nd French Armored Division to "liberate" Paris. This was a political decision upon which rested the future of de Gaulle's regime. Moreover, Leclerc and his officers tended to believe that their judgments about military operations were often superior to that of Americans.

Patton and Haislip had fought in France in World War I and attended French military schools. They spoke French and admired French culture. Their appreciation of France's proud military traditions helped them deal with Leclerc.

In his report on the Battle of Normandy, Eisenhower claimed that the equivalent of five panzer divisions had been destroyed. He admitted that a substantial number of enemy soldiers managed to get away: "The enemy employed great cleverness and skill in organizing a system of ferries and pontoon bridges over the Seine." Some pontoon bridges were concealed under camouflage along river banks in daylight, then swung across the stream at night. Having occupied the region for five years, the Germans knew the locations of the best places to ford the river.

By the 25th of August, 400,000 German soldiers had been killed or captured in battles in France. German armies lost 1300 tanks, 20,000 motor vehicles, 500 assault guns and 1500 field guns.[22]

With German forces in retreat, their grip on France relaxed in the last weeks of August. The world waited for news that Allied armies had crossed the Seine and liberated Paris.

7

The Third Army Crosses the Seine

When Patton ordered XV Corps to send a force to cross the Seine, Haislip selected the 79th Infantry and 5th Armored Divisions to execute the mission. On August 15 this task force approached Dreux, 40 miles west of Paris. With XV Corps also engaged northeast of Argentan, Patton commanded widely-separated corps. XII Corps advanced in the Orléans area. XX Corps captured Chartres on August 17 after some hard fighting. VIII Corps cleared pockets of resistance in Brittany and prepared to take Brest.

The Allies' supply situation was becoming critical. C-47s began to bring supplies to an airfield near Le Mans. It was the start of a daily emergency airlift to the Third Army.

On August 19, the 79th Division approached the Seine. Patton sent a message to Haislip: "Cross Seine River at Mantes-Gassicourt tonight 19–20 August 1944. Secure bridgehead. Send 5th Armored Division downstream repeat downstream to point twenty-five (25) miles below Mantes-Gassicourt. Cut crossings over Seine River."[1]

The 362nd Fighter Group dropped six-hour delay bombs on three ferry sites near Rouen to slow German movements across the Seine at night.[2] Patton asked Weyland to send reconnaissance airplanes to determine the condition of bridges upstream from Paris. A pilot of the 15th Reconnaissance Squadron flew along a 20-mile stretch of the river twice at 2500 feet on August 20 to photograph the bridges. These pictures helped the Third Army plan Seine crossings.[3]

Hundreds of barges used the Seine to bring cargoes to Paris. During the German retreat they carried vehicles and thousands of soldiers across the river. Allied aircraft attacked over 300 barges in the last week of August. XIX TAC's P-47s cooperated with XV Corps near Mantes by attacking tanks that disrupted the 79th Division's efforts to secure a bridgehead.[4]

The 79th Division crossed the Seine in what Haislip called "a lulu

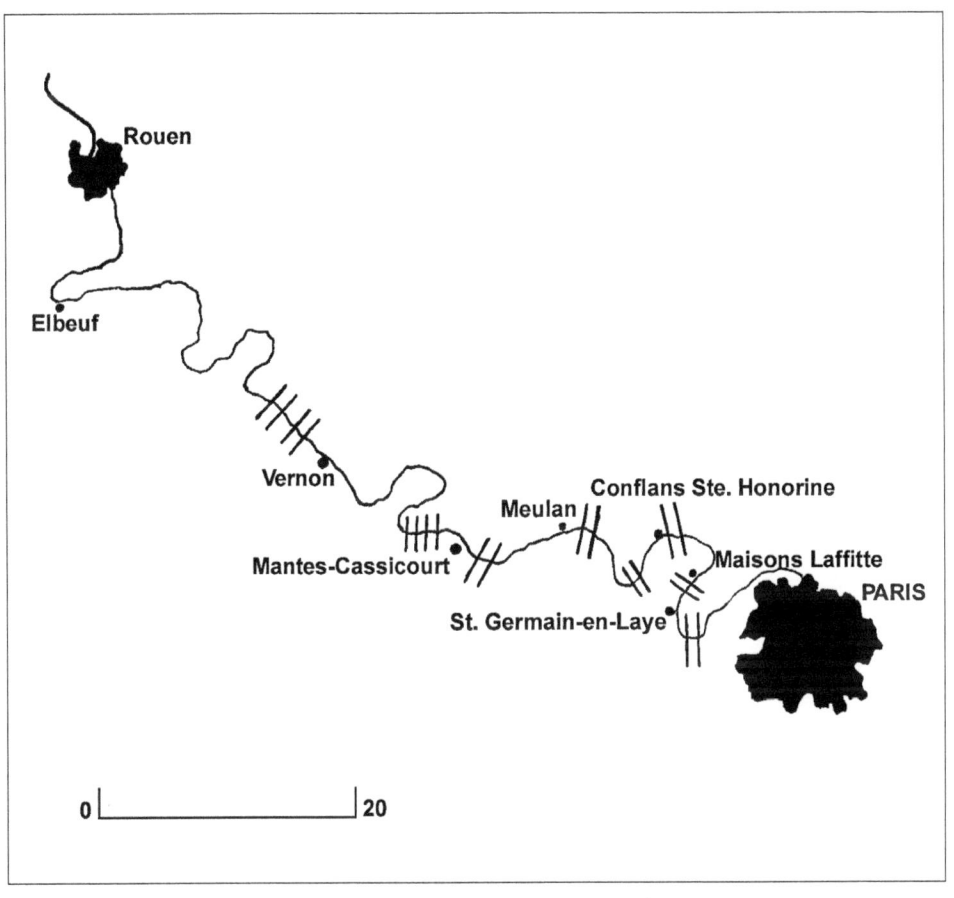

Map 4. Major Ferries on the Seine River, August 1944

of an operation." One regiment crossed the river at night in a torrential rainstorm, single-file along a footpath on a dam. The next day another regiment paddled over in assault boats. A third crossed in the afternoon on a treadway bridge constructed by division engineers.[5]

The 79th Division established a firm bridgehead on the east bank near Mantes, repelled counterattacks, and captured the headquarters of German Army Group B. Haislip sent the 5th Armored Division downstream to cut German escape routes.

In the region between Mantes and Rouen, the Seine had many ferry slips. German soldiers crossed the river on rafts, barges, small boats, and inflated tire tubes or anything else that would help keep them afloat.[6]

German commanders saw the danger of entrapment and fought hard to delay the 5th Armored. In four days the 5th advanced only 20 miles downstream. On August 24 it became part of the First Army.

XIX TAC's pilots reported that the main highways east of Paris were full of German vehicles.

Patton's troops scrounged to keep moving. They used captured German materials. Patton told his subordinates the story about a tramp who asked a housewife for a stone to make soup. Fascinated, she gave him a stone. He then asked for some carrots, then some potatoes, until soon he had ingredients for a nourishing soup. Patton felt like that tramp as he pleaded with SHAEF for more supplies.

When XV Corps secured a bridgehead across the Seine at Mantes, Bradley saw an opportunity to cut off German forces. He proposed that the British Second Army send several divisions through American positions to push downstream. General Dempsey rejected the suggestion.

Confusion developed among Allied forces as some U.S. units moved through territory assigned to the British. Bradley resented a claim made by Dempsey that the British Second Army had been delayed 48 hours by U.S. forces in its sector. Bradley pointed out that the First Army's drive to Elbeuf removed enemy forces from Dempsey's front and thereby helped the British advance.[7]

In the last week of August, German troops west of the Seine faced entrapment. Many waited with exemplary discipline to cross the wide part of the river between Elbeuf and Le Havre.

Elements of at least thirty-two German divisions retreated across the Seine in August. Disorganized, understrength, harassed frequently by aircraft and artillery, dependent on food growing locally to supplement meager rations, a substantial number of them escaped capture.[8] By intense effort, the Germans kept a few bridges open. More than half the vehicles and men that crossed the river did so over these structures.

A panzer officer, Colonel Hans von Luck, received orders from his division commander on August 21: "From now on you are on your own. I can't tell you where you will get fuel, ammunition, and food." Von Luck crossed the river in a Volkswagen amphibious car covered with brush. It floated 15 km downstream before he found a flat spot on a bank of the river near Rouen.[9]

A U.S. Army history concludes: "Despite serious losses, the Germans had extricated fighting men of good quality. It was the security troops, the antiaircraft personnel and the supply forces who filled the American prisoner cages, not the combat soldiers...."[10]

Weather helped German forces in retreat. During the second half of August, clouds and rain often hampered air operations.

The list below summarizes German losses during the retreat to the Seine in August:

1. Strength of German Divisions in Normandy: 300,000 men, 47,000 motor vehicles, 800 tanks
2. Reached the Seine: 240,000 men, 37,000 motor vehicles, 190 tanks
3. Crossed the Seine: 225,000 men, 33,000 motor vehicles, 130 tanks

Tank losses were high. It was difficult to determine why crews abandoned tanks. Fires and explosions caused by air attacks and artillery, traffic jams, casualties, lack of fuel, impassable bridges, mechanical breakdowns, and disrupted railroads were some of the causes.[11]

Some panzer soldiers may have concluded that tanks would probably not survive a 300-mile march to Germany even if they could find fuel or railroad lines in operation.

In May 1944, Allied air forces started a trial bombing campaign against German oil installations. Heavy bombers struck oil refineries during the next few weeks. ULTRA and other intelligence sources provided evidence that fuel shortages were beginning to cripple the German war effort. On June 8 General Spaatz made oil a primary objective for strategic bombing. German forces in Normandy began to feel the effects of an oil shortage just when they needed fuel to move troops and vehicles to the east.[12]

An AAF air campaign conducted prior to the invasion of Normandy had destroyed most railroad bridges and many road bridges on the Seine.

A large number of German soldiers crossed the Seine on August 26–27. Eighteen major ferries operated, and a bridge near Rouen was passable. A U.S. Army history records that German commanders later expressed the opinion that, "...the British and Canadian forces did not push as hard as they might have. Neither did the Allied air forces seem as active as usual during the critical days of the withdrawal."[13] SHAEF had assumed incorrectly that there were few Germans remaining west of the Seine.

German engineers improvised ways to keep bridges and ferries in operation. A bridge near Rouen consisted of a long pontoon which pivoted on a piling in the center of the river. It rotated to one side of the river to load troops and equipment, then to the other side to debark them. Some pontoon bridge sections were towed to banks to be concealed on clear days. About 16,000 vehicles crossed over a bridge near Elbeuf between August 19 and 24.

Thousands of German soldiers crossed the Seine over bridges at St. Germain-en-Laye and Maisons Laffitte, most of them on the night of August 24–25. Both German and Allied commanders had decided not to destroy bridges in the Paris area.[14]

Bombed bridge at Mantes-Gassicourt (courtesy of USAFHRA).

Since the middle of August, any one of three U.S. corps could have liberated Paris. Eisenhower was not eager to order such a move. It would have negative consequences:

1. Civilians in Paris would need supplies.
2. A battle for the city could damage priceless cultural treasures.
3. Operations to free Paris would divert Allied forces from more important missions.

The staff of Communications Zone ETO [Com Z], the unit responsible for supplying U.S. armies, had mixed feelings about Paris. Its capture would force Com Z to bring food, coal, medicines and other vital materials to the city using a transportation system already strained to its breaking point. On the other hand, Paris was the center of rail, road and communications networks that Com Z needed. Eisenhower hoped to delay the liberation of Paris, but the world waited for this dramatic event, and de Gaulle's group urged that it take place soon.

On August 7 Hitler appointed General Dietrich von Choltitz to command Greater Paris and to defend it using whatever measures were necessary. He ordered von Choltitz to stamp out any resistance from French civilians without mercy, and to make certain the city was a "field of ruins" before it was abandoned to the Allies.

It was not likely that the Germans could keep Paris quiet. Already, as Patton's troops occupied positions on the Seine above and below the city, strikes, attacks on German soldiers, anti–German demonstrations and other evidence of insurrection appeared. Gas, water and electric power services were sharply cut.

De Gaulle urged the Resistance to cease aggressive actions. The thing he feared most was a violent uprising in Paris that might result in a seizure of power by communists.

Undisciplined groups roamed the city, claiming to be part of the Resistance, taking orders from no one. Harassment of the few remaining German troops increased.

On August 19 von Choltitz entered negotiations with French Resistance leaders to establish a truce. He had little choice. He knew he could not effectively defend Paris against both Allied armies and Parisians in revolt.

Von Choltitz decided to disobey Hitler's orders. He would not crush civilian opposition in Paris with executions, and he would not order unnecessary destruction of property. These were courageous and historic decisions, especially since some German generals who failed to obey Hitler's orders were executed or forced to commit suicide.[15]

De Gaulle continued to badger Eisenhower to send Allied forces to Paris, led by the 2nd French Armored Division. Leclerc, whose division was now part of the First Army, sent a small force to approach Paris on 21 August, despite an order from his corps commander not to do so. Eisenhower recognized that the situation was getting out of control. He summarized the situation in a letter to Marshall: "If the enemy tries to hold Paris with any real strength he would be a constant menace to our flank. If he largely concedes the place, it falls into our hands whether we like it or not."[16]

With bitter humor, Bradley suggested that Paris could be liberated by the hordes of newspaper reporters pleading to go to the city. Reluctantly, he directed the 2nd French Armored Division to enter Paris.

Leclerc's troops moved slowly through crowds of delirious civilians wishing to salute their liberators. Impatient to get the liberation of Paris finished, Bradley ordered the 4th Infantry Division to enter the city, "and to hell with [French] prestige."[17]

Von Choltitz ordered his troops to withdraw during the night of August 24–25. During that night, a small force of the 2nd French Armored Division entered Paris. Shortly thereafter, elements of the 4th Division moved into Paris and occupied the plaza in front of Notre Dame cathedral.

De Gaulle arrived in Paris on August 25 to establish a government. Random shots continued to ring out around the city, fired for no apparent reason. The next day de Gaulle led a parade down the Champs-Elysées.

Eisenhower and Bradley went to Paris on August 26. Montgomery refused an invitation to join them. He was too busy, he explained.

The people of Paris appeared cheerful, healthy and eager to celebrate. De Gaulle told Eisenhower that the appearances were deceptive. He claimed the city had only one day's supply of food on hand, and "the lack of coal is grave." SHAEF organized an airlift of supplies to Paris.

The 2nd French Armored Division was not eager to leave Paris. It remained in the capital for weeks to help de Gaulle's organization take control of France's government.

Allied engineers gave priority to rehabilitation of airfields in the Paris area for transport aircraft and bombers. They brought 3000 tons of supplies a day for the city. The British assigned 179 trucks with trailers to bring supplies from the coast. The 12th Army Group sent 60,000 gallons of fuel and 6000 gallons of lubricants to Paris each day. On battle fronts to the east of Paris, Allied commanders complained about opportunities lost for lack of fuel.[18]

The day Paris was liberated was also a memorable day for the Eighth and Ninth Air Forces. Their fighters and fighter-bombers destroyed 90 German aircraft in strafing attacks on airfields east of Paris. XIX TAC flew more than 12,000 sorties in August. It destroyed the following:

4058 water vessels	2956 railroad cars
466 tanks and armored vehicles	18 merchant ships
596 horse-drawn wagons	8 naval vessels
246 locomotives	229 aircraft

This was only part of XIX TAC's August efforts. It also attacked gun positions, ammunition and supply dumps, troop concentrations, railroad yards, and railroad tracks. Its reconnaissance operations were especially useful during this period, when German forces retreated in daylight.[19]

In late August, XIX TAC accelerated moves to airfields east of Paris. The GAF attacked Allied aircraft occasionally. On August 19 a squadron of the 406th Fighter Group was bounced by more than 40 fighters near Pontoise and lost five P-47s.

On August 25 Patton sent a message to Weyland containing high praise for XIX TAC:

> The superior efficiency and cooperation afforded this Army by the forces under your command are the best examples of the combined use of air and ground troops I have ever witnessed.
>
> Due to the tireless efforts of your flyers large movements of hostile vehicles and troop concentrations ahead of our advancing columns have been harassed or obliterated. The information passed directly to heads of the columns from the air has saved time and lives.
>
> I am voicing the opinion of all the officers and men in this Army when I express to you our admiration and appreciation of your magnificent efforts.[20]

Despite heavy losses, the German retreat across the Seine was a significant achievement. It was helped by bad weather, diversion of Allied resources to the civilians of Paris, and an Allied supply crisis. In early September, at a critical time in operations, Eisenhower assumed control of Allied ground operations. This led to some command confusion. The timing of the change was motivated in large part by pointed suggestions from the War Department. U.S. newspapers and politicians were asking why Montgomery retained authority over American ground forces.

Optimism spread throughout Allied forces in early September about the possibility of an end of the war with Germany. Eisenhower urged his subordinates to take exceptional risks and push hard at enemy forces that seemed to be near collapse. A logistics crisis, however, began to weaken Allied efforts.

The Drive to the Meuse

After the capture of Angers, Patton sent the 5th Division south of Le Mans "to guard against a very doubtful attack on our [south] flank." XX Corps now had the 7th Armored Division and the 35th, 80th and 5th Infantry Divisions. Walker sent XX Corps driving eastward, with inevitable breakdowns in communications. The commander of the 5th Division recorded that orders "made no sense at all." Confused or not, the 5th Division moved against light Opposition, and by August 16 it had entered the outskirts of Chartres.[1]

The 7th Armored Division reached Chartres on the night of August 15. German troops fought hard to delay the Americans. To seize a foothold in the city, Walker sent a combat team of the 5th Division to help the 7th Armored. A group of 800 German soldiers surrendered en masse. XX Corps' artillery gave excellent support to armor and infantry in the battle. Two staff officers of XX Corps were killed while making a reconnaissance in Chartres.[2]

The 5th Division's llth Regiment marched eastward from Milly on August 23 to take Fontainebleau and seize a bridge over the Seine. Advance elements reached the bridge only a few minutes after the Germans demolished it.

A battalion commander conducted a reconnaissance along the river and located five small boats which a platoon used to cross the river. Other soldiers waded or swam across.

Throughout the night of August 23, Germans attacked the small bridgehead. Each time, artillery, mortar and small-arms fire drove them back. Heavy rain began shortly after midnight and slowed the fighting. Americans built up a bridgehead while blunting enemy attacks. By 1630 hours, engineers finished a treadway bridge. It became evident by 2000 hours that the Germans had started to withdraw.

On August 26 Walker ordered armored units to drive toward the Marne River. To a World War I veteran like Walker, this river brought back many memories. Two days later XX Corps crossed the Marne.

The 5th Division took Reims on August 29 and captured an airplane factory, an ordnance depot, many supply depots and stocks of champagne and brandy.

German forces had difficulty adjusting to the tactics of the XX Corps, which bypassed towns and strong points, then later attacked them from the east. In August, XX Corps' headquarters changed positions fourteen times.[3]

Patton ordered XII Corps to take Orléans, a key city on the Loire which gave its name to a geographical gap with extensive road and rail connections to eastern France. On August 15 Major General Gilbert Cook, XII Corps' commander, sent a task force comprised of elements of the 35th Infantry and 4th Armored Divisions to take Orléans. Poor communications caused some command confusion. Cook received instructions to take Châteaudun too, but he did not let this order distract him from his main objective. XII Corps would take Châteaudun after Orléans.

When the 4th Armored Division received orders to take Orléans, it had just completed a 167-mile march and expected to take a week's rest. But both Cook and the 4th Armored commander, General Wood, believed that speed at this stage of the campaign would bring great rewards and reduce casualties. Wood ordered CCA of the 4th Armored Division to drive toward Orléans. It was a march into the unknown. CCA had four Michelin tourist maps to guide it. Little reliable intelligence was available about German dispositions, strength and intentions. Information provided by French civilians was often unreliable. The CCA commander, Colonel Bruce Clarke, believed that civilians often overestimated German strength.

Clarke was a tank commander in the pattern of Patton, Cook and Wood. He believed that mobility and firepower were the greatest assets of an armored force. Never stop when in pursuit of an enemy. There are always good reasons to pause, but to relax pressure gives the enemy time to set mines and strengthen his defenses. Clarke told his staff that, "If you can keep a German from planning, you've got him." Armor should punch through the enemy's front and rampage through his rear, destroying communications and spreading panic.[4]

Like Patton, the 4th Armored's leaders did not worry unduly about enemy threats to the division's rear and flanks. A 4th Armored boast expressed this attitude: "They've got us surrounded again, the poor bastards."

On the night of August 15, a XII Corps task force captured an airport near Orléans. Within a few days, fighter-bombers and transports began using it. The next day two columns of armor, supported by infantry and artillery, seized Orléans against light opposition. The speed of XII Corps' attack dashed any German hopes to hold the Orléans gap.

Cook sent an infantry regiment to take Châteaudun on August 17. After some sharp fighting it overcame opposition from a few hundred German troops.

The 4th Armored Division had trained for two years before it landed on Normandy beaches 36 days after D-Day. In its first operations it cleared the way through Avranches for the Third Army, cleared Rennes, seized Vannes, and moved toward Lorient. Allied leaders decided that the port of Lorient should be contained, not assaulted.

Under Wood's leadership the 4th Armored Division fought like a cavalry outfit. Reconnaissance teams roamed to its front until they met resistance too strong to eliminate. If the position could not be safely bypassed, it was attacked by various combinations of tanks, armored infantry, mobile artillery and fighter-bombers. Wood believed it was a misuse of armor to get bogged down in a static battle against enemy forces holding defensive positions too strong for an armored division. Its best role was to slice through the enemy's front into his rear, cutting communications and creating disorder.

The 4th Armored was a mobile powerhouse, with 263 tanks, three armored infantry battalions carried in half-track vehicles, and three mobile artillery battalions armed with 105 mm howitzers. Truck convoys rolled night and day to bring the division food, fuel and ammunition. It often assigned its three combat commands separate tasks. Flexibility characterized the 4th Armored's organization.

Wood used a liaison airplane to check the progress of his division. Pennants waved from the wings of his Grasshopper as it landed on a road or field for a conference with his task force leaders.[5]

The major armored weapon of American armored divisions was the Sherman M-4 medium tank. It weighed 35 tons, carried a 5-man crew, and fired a 75 mm gun with a relatively low muzzle velocity. It was inferior to German Tiger and Panther tanks in armor and fire power. It had a dependable engine and its rubber-block tracks lasted five times longer than tracks of German tanks. To retain numerical superiority, the American army put heavy emphasis on tank maintenance and recovery of damaged armored vehicles.

Combat Command A of the 4th Armored rested a few days near Orléans to rearm and refuel. On August 21 it seized Sens, a city 35 miles west of Troyes, where it captured 30 carloads of gasoline and 300 tons of food. These acquisitions eased the shortages that became serious as XII Corps stretched its supply lines.

M-4 Sherman tank (courtesy of the Patton Museum).

On August 24, CCA received orders to take Troyes, a historic city on the Seine 90 miles southeast of Paris. Intelligence reports estimated that 500 German service troops occupied Troyes. At 1700 a task force of CCA charged three and a half miles across an open plain northwest of Troyes. This force, composed of medium tanks, armored infantry in half-tracks, and self-propelled howitzers, fought its way into the city through intense artillery and anti-tank fire. Allied intelligence reports on Troyes had been wrong. Approximately 3000 German soldiers held the city. By nightfall, CCA troops reached the city center. Armored infantry fought house-to-house to eliminate panzerfausts (similar to bazookas) and wipe out anti-tank crews. The next day CCA secured half of Troyes. German troops began to withdraw. Remaining pockets of resistance were cleared by early afternoon of August 26. In defense of Troyes, German forces lost 533 men killed and 573 captured.[6]

The American assault on Troyes challenged a U.S. Army guideline that tanks should not be used in towns. The 4th Armored Division demonstrated that a balanced force of tanks, infantry, artillery and engineers could break into a built-up area, providing it gave the enemy little time

Trucks of the 4th Armored Division passing damaged German equipment (courtesy of USAMHI).

to prepare strong defenses. Tanks should move through alleyways and back yards rather than main streets. After penetrating into the city for three or four blocks on a narrow front, the armored force can attack in several directions.

After the capture of Troyes, the XII Corps commander sent a commendation to the 4th Armored: "Another job quickly and well done. So far your command has been the spearhead of the corps, which today is leading all others in the advance to the east." [7]

CCA pursued German forces across the Marne River at Vitry-le-François and cut roads east of Châlons-sur-Marne. Both cities were cleared of Germans by August 29. As August ended, the 4th Armored Division smashed into Commercy on the Meuse River and captured a bridge intact.

In its operations in France in the summer of 1944, 4th Armored Division engineers always stayed near leading elements, with bridging and mine-clearing equipment to help tanks keep moving. Stalled vehicles were not allowed to block traffic. Slowing down or stopping was often more dangerous than rolling fast. Supply trucks were critical to the division's mobility. Like aircraft, tanks lose most of their value without fuel, ammunition and maintenance. Trucks mounted .50 caliber machine guns because they were sometimes attacked in regions not yet entirely cleared of enemy troops. Tanks carried their ammunition. Crews used it prudently. They did not want to be without shells when they encountered enemy armor.

In four weeks the 4th Armored Division had led XII Corps across France to the banks of the Meuse, through World War I battlegrounds at Verdun, St. Mihiel and the Argonne Forest. During this period, the division's trucks logged more than 3000 miles. At the Meuse the drive ended. A 4th Armored Division officer later wrote:

> This was the end of the line — out of maps and out of gas, the command [CCA] was to remain in this position until 12 September. The road was clear ahead, the Moselle River was still undefended and the road to Germany was open but even the most willing hands cannot drag a Sherman tank. This enforced delay was to cause us much suffering and many casualties in the coming months.[8]

At SHAEF and the 21st Army Group some staff officers resented Patton's criticism of their performance. They believed that the Third Army had to be halted. Supply services could not support offensives on the entire front in September. Eisenhower, prodded by Montgomery, would have to make some difficult decisions to cope with the logistics crisis, decisions which would infuriate Patton and Bradley.

9

The Capture of Brest

Soon after the Third Army became operational on August 1, the 6th Armored Division drove west through Brittany to the outskirts of Brest. Major General Grow, the division commander, called it the greatest cavalry-type operation of the war. Perhaps it was, but the division failed to seize its major objective—the port of Brest. The German commander refused to surrender, and Grow did not have a force strong enough to assault the massive fortifications guarding the port.

In the last days of August, only a month of moderate summer weather remained before autumn storms curtailed air operations and unloading of supplies across Normandy beaches. Allied forces needed more ports to supply combat units with ammunition, fuel, rations and equipment. Abundant supplies were available in the U.K., U.S., and on ships anchored in the Channel. To deliver them to the troops, Com Z needed not only ports, but also roads, railroads and airfields in France.

Eisenhower decided that Brest would have to be taken. It was a major port. Nevertheless, the decision is puzzling. As Early as September 1 it seemed certain that Allied armies would soon be within a day's march of the German border. This meant that supplies from Brest would have to travel 400 miles over demolished French roads, railroads, and bridges to reach front lines. Until rail lines were restored to service, trucks would be the primary means to carry supplies to the armies, but they consumed substantial quantities of scarce gasoline on their round trips. Many of the loads they carried were reduced by pilferage.

Allied armies needed large amounts of material to function effectively. Combat aircraft were useless without ammunition, fuel, and airfields. They consumed prodigious amounts of high-octane gasoline. Engineers needed construction materials. Allied supply services could not satisfy these requirements in August and September at a level which would permit combat forces to operate at full strength. This failure had tragic consequences. General Patton called it the "momentous error of the war."

Eisenhower told Middleton to take Brest without incurring excessive casualties. This meant that VIII Corps would receive large amounts of artillery, air, naval and transportation support during a critical period when weather was most suitable for air and ground operations in eastern France. When the assault on Brest began on August 25, a major part of the Third Army was 280 miles east of Brest.

The Ninth Air Force gave high priority to Brest operations. XIX TAC provided most of the fighter-bomber support.

The supply crisis that motivated the Brest operation also handicapped it. General Middleton complained about shortages of artillery ammunition. He had 31 battalions of artillery but not enough shells for them. He also criticized air support, "which left much to be desired." Bradley decided to increase support for VIII Corps. On September 8 substantial amounts of ammunition arrived. The next day American soldiers fought their way into Brest's outer fortifications.

Flak around Brest was intense. The 362nd Fighter Group reported that, "milling around at low altitude, often under a low cloud cover, right over the enemy front lines ... was perhaps the most grueling work the pilots ever did." This group bombed ships in the harbor, an action of questionable value since the Allies hoped to use the port soon.[1]

Many roads in the Brest area were sunken and bordered by hedgerows. German soldiers dug slots in the hedgerows for firing positions. They had concrete bunkers nearby in which they sheltered during artillery and air attacks.

Antitank guns had wide fields of fire. Roads were mined, some with 300-pound naval shells.

Forts, situated on high ground, had earth-filled, stone-faced walls 40 feet thick. Wide moats surrounded the forts.

To attack forts, infantry moved through minefields under cover of smoke. Tanks spewed flaming fuel at forts while 105 mm howitzers fired pointblank at gates. Engineers cleared mines and filled moats.

Much of this weaponry did not touch defenders in their underground, reinforced-concrete shelters.

Fierce and costly combat continued until September 18 when the German commander surrendered his force of 38,000 soldiers. When Brest fell, VIII Corps had 25,000 tons of ammunition in its supply dumps.[2]

The Brest campaign has received much criticism. U.S. Army historians concluded that, "Poor communications, long distances and weather contributed their adverse effects, but at the bottom of the difficulties was improper co-ordination ... at all echelons of higher command due to the optimistic initial belief that Brest would fall quickly."[3] This conclusion avoids the main issue and administers a slap to General Patton, who did say that Brest would be captured quickly.

Basically, the Brest assault was ill-advised because the port could not be used for many months after it was taken, if at all, and it was hundreds of miles from Allied front lines. These facts should have been apparent to SHAEF's staff.

The AAF gave Brest operations a vast amount of support. Its efforts, too, have been sharply criticized. An AAF history described the Brest campaign as a "strange and highly individual story, marred by poor air-ground cooperation and much waste of air power."[4] Vandenberg reported that after one intense attack by the Ninth Air Force on Brest, a commander of ground forces complained that they were not ready for the air effort and could not take advantage of it. The Ninth Air Force gave the assault on Brest its highest priority in September. XIX TAC and other Allied air units, including heavy and medium bomber groups, diverted resources from other operations to help VIII Corps capture Brest.[5]

A period of intense air effort in support of operations at Brest began on September 5. On this day alone, XIX TAC employed seven fighter-bomber groups plus five more from IX TAC. On 554 sorties, fighter-bombers dropped 199 tons of general purpose bombs, 65 tons of fragmentation bombs and 108 tanks of Napalm.[6]

Poor intelligence hampered air operations. Targets for fighter-bomber attacks were often unsuitable. Ground forces had little knowledge of the capabilities and limitations of air power. Most ground units lacked air liaison officers to advise their commanders.

Brest and its surrounding forts were defended by a German garrison whose commander was determined to hold out as long as possible and to demolish the port before capitulation. The defenders had a variety of effective antiaircraft weapons.[7]

In the period of September 3 to 14, XIX TAC's fighter-bombers attacked gun positions, buildings, ammunition dumps, fuel dumps, motor vehicles, naval vessels and coastal batteries. Heavy and medium bombers bombed fortifications with poor results; bombs did little damage to massive stone walls.

Not all air effort was wasted. Fighter-bombers sometimes placed their bombs in the right places at the right times. When aircraft were overhead, German artillery remained quiet, and soldiers stayed in their bunkers. Ground attacks were more likely to be successful when they began soon after air attacks ended.[8]

A few weeks after the surrender, the Ninth Air Force ORS analyzed the air effort expended on Brest and issued a scathing report:

9. The Capture of Brest

The underlying reason for the apparent misuse of air power, 4–5 September 1944, particularly for the heavy and medium bomber attacks, may be laid to the under-estimation of the entire strength of the defenses of Brest. There were too few Air Corps officers assigned to VIII Corps who were familiar with the effects of bombing attacks, fuzings, and close support.[9]

The report claimed that heavy bombers "are of so little tactical value [against targets like those in Brest] that they should not be used. The use of medium bombers other than [in] attacks upon open gun positions has proved to be useless. If aircraft are used to support an assault by ground forces, the highest kind of cooperation and communication is necessary between air, infantry and artillery."

ORS analysts reported an amazing achievement: "During the entire operation against Fortress Brest, no casualties to Allied ground personnel were caused by friendly planes." Airmen made "sparing" use of napalm because of the "inaccurate trajectory of this weapon."

Air planning was sometimes lax. When pilots neared their targets, conditions had often changed so much that plans made 15 to 24 hours previously were obsolete.

Soldiers of the divisions that assaulted Brest praised the air support they received. They reported that fighter-bombers operating in direct support of ground troops were absolutely essential to successful attacks on strongpoints.[10]

Reports like this should not be accepted at face value. Ground commanders usually praised air efforts so as not to give air forces a reason to reject future requests for help. Although air attacks did not achieve all that the AAF hoped for, they did disrupt communications, silence artillery, and force troops to seek cover.

A major problem with all tactical air operations was inappropriate setting of bomb fuses. It is critical to set a bomb's fuse so that its force is directed at vulnerable parts of its target.

An AAF history expresses strong disapproval of Brest operations: communications facilities were "markedly deficient, air-ground coordination abysmal, and intelligence ... sketchy.... On too many occasions air was asked to bomb invulnerable targets. Too frequently bombs of the wrong size and fuzing were used."[11]

With the conquest of Brest, Allied forces captured a demolished city and port. Even before the German capitulation, SHAEF decided that the port was almost useless. It would take too long to repair its facilities. The harbor could only be used with locks, but these were wrecked.

SHAEF decided not to try to capture other port cities in Brittany, such as Lorient, St. Nazaire, and Nantes. Their garrisons would be contained by minimal forces.

It is somewhat strange that Allied planners did not anticipate that the port could not be used for many months after its capture. Brest must have been familiar to thousands of regular U.S. Army officers. It had served as a major port of entry for American soldiers in World War 1.

Middleton told a biographer: "When the city fell, I found that the harbor had silted up from the flow of the rivers. Our air and artillery ... had sunk ships in the harbor — it was full of sunken ships."[12]

Neither Bradley nor Eisenhower ever conceded that Brest had been a pointless, wasteful campaign, one that consumed resources at a time when Allied forces could have advanced to the German frontier if they had received enough supplies.

Patton recalled that Eisenhower told him: "[General] Lee and the Communications Zone have done a marvelous job," Patton disagreed: "...we consider that they have failed utterly and probably lost a victory before winter through their inability to keep us supplied with gasoline."[13]

Bradley gave the following explanation for the Brest campaign: "To have contained [German forces in Brest] would have required more troops than we could spare...."[14]

Patton recorded a statement by Bradley even stranger than the one just cited: "We must take Brest in order to maintain the illusion of the fact that the U.S. Army cannot be beaten."[15]

No amount of rationalization can soften or excuse the facts: 50,000 U.S. troops fought a bitter battle lasting a month, during a critical period, to capture a port 400 miles from the Third Army's front lines, a port that was demolished.

Patton excoriated the Allied supply organization for its alleged failures in the summer of 1944, but COM Z had many accomplishments. In mid–September, despite lack of a major port in working condition, 16 U.S. divisions were supplied 200 miles beyond the Seine. Two other divisions, fighting hard in Brittany, received strong logistics support.

It was not Com Z's responsibility to capture ports. Com Z did not demolish railroad centers, tracks, bridges and roads in many parts of France. Many of the decisions that brought about the logistics crisis were made at SHAEF.

An AAF history describes the railroad chaos in France: "The use of rail transportation was greatly hampered and delayed by the extensive dislocation of the French and Belgium rail systems caused by Allied bombings."[16] Eisenhower made the decision to launch this air assault in the months before the Normandy invasion. AAF commanders denounced the campaign, and they were joined by many experts on railroad operations. They believed that bombing railroad centers could not achieve its purpose — to block German military traffic to the Normandy lodgment area. As it turned out, the doubters were right. Bombing rail centers did not prevent Germans from building up a force in Normandy that held Allied forces at a relatively small beachhead for more than six weeks. Too slowly, and too late, it became evident that Allied air forces, with their overwhelming air superiority, could slow German troop and supply movements without demolishing French and Belgian transportation systems.

A U.S. Army history claims that Eisenhower's decisions were not responsible for the logistics crisis. Conditions beyond his control forced his hand: "The build-up of men and certain critical supplies in the United Kingdom, the arrival of divisions in France, the requisition and transport of civil supplies, the organization of military government, the rebuilding of rail lines, the laying of pipe lines—virtually the whole intricate military machine was geared to a slower rate of advance than was required in late August."[17] Nevertheless, it was SHAEF's responsibility to insure that supplies were available to the armies so that they could exploit offensive opportunities.

The slow progress of Allied armies in June and July was evidently not exploited by COM Z to prepare for offensives such as the one the Third Army executed in August. Logistics planning had lulled COM Z into complacency. On the 98th day after D-Day in Normandy, Allied armies had advanced to a line which planners had forecast would take them 350 days to reach.

Beach unloading saved Allied forces from a virtual strangulation of supply services. When complicated cargo-handling systems proved to be inefficient, sailors and soldiers on the beaches improvised solutions. One such improvisation helped enormously: seamen learned to beach landing craft at low tide, something the Navy had forbidden. This made it possible to unload cargoes directly on shore, thereby dispensing with floating piers, pontoon causeways and several loading-unloading steps.[18]

At the end of August, Bradley gave some bad news to Patton. Supplies for the Third Army would have to be cut again. Eisenhower decided that offensives in the American sectors would have to be postponed until ports were captured on the Channel. He had his eye on Antwerp. An assault on Germany's heartland could be supported most efficiently from the Channel ports of France, the Netherlands and Belgium. Montgomery's 21st Army Group would receive priority on supplies to support offensives toward Antwerp. The First Army would receive sufficient supplies to enable it to support the 21st Army Group's offensives.

Patton expressed his disgust: "We got no gas.... British have put it over again to suit Monty, the First Army must get most of it, and we are also feeding the Parisians. It is a terrible mistake, and when it comes out in the after years, it will cause much argument.... We should cross the Rhine ... and the faster we do it the less lives and munitions it will take."[19]

On August 29 the Third Army received 80,000 gallons of gasoline; its average daily allowance was 400,000 gallons.

A history of U.S. Army supply services in World War II supports Patton's charges about Com Z. It claims that conservatism and pessimism of OVERLORD's logisticians was a root cause of the supply crisis. The author called support for Allied drives in the summer of 1944 "an exercise in logistics pusillanimity unparalleled in modern war." The book reminds us that the Allies had a large number of vehicles, air supremacy, and a friendly population. "Yet for all these advantages, the Allied offensive had to be carried out against the logistician's advice."[20] Roads and railroads were in bad condition, but a determined effort made after SHAEF acknowledged the seriousness of the supply situation reclaimed enough of them to use exclusively to supply the armies.

Estimates of logistics planners were often highly conservative. They estimated that trucks could not drive more than 1000 miles per day, but during the supply crisis they exceeded that figure. Moreover, they carried heavier loads than guidelines recommended. Allied logisticians also overestimated the amounts of fuel needed by tanks in pursuit operations.

Eisenhower believed that SHAEF had to send food, medicines and fuel to Paris. During operations in North Africa his relations with French officials had been widely criticized. This experience and subsequent disagreements with French leaders made him reluctant to reject requests from de Gaulle. Moreover, he wanted to avoid antagonizing the French people and Francophiles around the world. He did not want to see any more newspaper articles critical of his decisions regarding the French.

Paris exerted a serious drain on Allied supplies and transportation. A U.S. Army history points out that Parisians had survived four years of German occupation, but now their needs for staples were suddenly "sufficiently urgent" to require 1500 tons per day, "regardless of the cost to the military effort." French civilians had received virtually no gasoline from the Germans, but now Com Z supplied 3000 tons of petroleum products each day for the Paris and Reims areas.[21]

Delivery of supplies to Paris also drained military transportation services and personnel. Trucks, airplanes, barges and railroads were used to carry goods to Paris.

On September 28 Eisenhower tried to calm an angry Bradley, who had been ordered by SHAEF to assign thirteen battalions for service on supply lines. Eisenhower explained: "We have had so much trouble with thievery and other difficulties that we simply must provide guards ... to protect our line of communications from the French...."[22]

The War Department complained forcefully about the slow unloading of cargo ships in France. Only 95 out of a scheduled 175 ships were unloaded on the Continent in September, and the situation worsened in October. This hurt the Allied war effort worldwide. Some planners in the War Department charged that Com Z had requested more matériel than U.S. armies in the ETO needed.[23]

Com Z operated its trucks 20 hours a day, seven days a week. This required a large personnel force. Com Z combed out army and air force units to find 5000 men to be trained as drivers. Eisenhower later recalled that the 2½-ton truck was a most valuable piece of military equipment, as were the jeep, the bulldozer, and the C-47 airplane. "Curiously enough," he wrote, "none of these is designed for combat."[24]

To cope with the supply crisis, the U.S. Army Transportation Corps organized a system called the Red Ball Express. On an average day, 900 vehicles traveled two one-way routes reserved for military transportation services. Personnel and vehicles were used to the limit of their endurance. By August 29, 132 truck companies, with a total of 5958 vehicles, were assigned to the project. Many army and air force units had to give up trucks to the Red Ball Express. Traffic control-points provided fuel, vehicle checks, rest and food for drivers. Military police directed traffic and tried to reduce pilferage. During the 81 days it operated, the Red Ball Express brought an average of 5088 tons of supplies a day to the fronts. As the runs increased to 600 miles, more mechanical breakdowns occurred. Vehicles were not serviced as often as they should have been.[25]

Motor vehicles are crucial to operations of tactical air forces. They move often and consume a great amount of matériel. The Ninth Air Force Service Command's truck companies traveled over six million miles in August and September to haul gasoline, ammunition and other goods to air groups. In August, when fighter-bombers flew four or five missions a day, the average daily consumption of gasoline per plane reached 350 gallons.[26]

AAF units had to transfer 600 vehicles to COM Z during the supply crisis. When air groups could not keep close to the armies they supported because of truck shortages or lack of airfields, their aircraft had to burn gasoline on long flights to and from the fronts. This also took a toll on equipment and pilots. It became difficult to maintain cover for armored columns. Two squadrons rotated to provide cover while a third was off operations for maintenance and repair of equipment.[27]

Gasoline trucks of the Red Ball Express (courtesy of USAMHI).

In August and September, the Third Army depended on trucks for most of its supplies. The Red Ball Express carried supplies from the Normandy coast to dumps near Reims, a round trip of 670 miles. Transport of supplies by truck had many drawbacks. Trucks were slow, uneconomical with fuel, and required a large personnel force to operate and guard them. Loading and unloading consumed great amounts of time and labor. They were vulnerable to thieves. The French black market had developed smooth techniques and efficient networks during the German occupation.

Railroad transportation avoids many of the negatives of trucking. A single train of fifty boxcars can carry more freight than several hundred trucks, and do it faster, more efficiently, and with fewer workers. Trains operate almost as safely at night as in daylight. They can be guarded effectively to prevent thefts. COM Z put equipment and personnel into a crash program to restore quickly at least a few railroad lines to service. Workers were recruited from the French population. Locomotives burned coal instead of scarce gasoline, but many had been damaged by Allied aircraft, sabotage or German demolitions. They had to be repaired. Allied armies captured coal mines in northern France and Belgium in September.

A history of the Ninth Air Force Service Command [AFSC] states that it operated as a "combination drug store, repair shop, gunsmith, warehouse, state university, parcel service, discount store, commercial pipeline, ambulance service, and personnel department."[28] One of its tasks was to assemble liaison airplanes that arrived in France in boxes. The fuselage and vertical tail were intact, but AFSC had to assemble wings, propeller, elevators and landing gear.

When aircraft were modified, and they often were, AFSC trained personnel to cope with the changes.

In late August, fuel pipelines were laid from the beaches to army depots in eastern France. By early October they delivered 4500 tons of gasoline daily to the armies.

A tug-of-war ensued between supply services and combat units. This tension became particularly acute in the airborne arm when transport aircraft were assigned to carry supplies. It was indicative of the seriousness of the supply crisis that SHAEF assigned transport aircraft and heavy bombers to carry gasoline and other materials to ground forces. This, of course, interfered with the combat missions of the airborne army and the strategic air forces.

It is one of the advantages of a military system which has a supreme commander that dispositions of forces can be changed promptly to meet changing conditions.

10

Air Supply for Ground Forces

Demolished roads and railroads, and a lack of ports in France, contributed to a critical supply shortage that hamstrung Allied armies in the autumn of 1944. To cope with the crisis, SHAEF ordered Allied air forces to increase air supply operations. All types of aircraft, including liaison planes, C-47s and bombers, were assigned to airlift missions. Aircraft of the First Allied Airborne Army [FAAA] flew supply missions when they could be relieved of their obligations to airborne forces. In response to an appeal from Eisenhower, Arnold combed out over 100 transports from units in the U.S. and sent them to Europe.

OVERLORD's planners had anticipated a need for airlifts, but not to the extent that became necessary. No central authority had been established to coordinate air supply services. In June, five distinct American air transport organizations existed in the ETO. Each reported to a different headquarters. By far the largest organization capable of executing supply airlifts was IX Troop Carrier Command [IX TCC], with 1400 transports.

Before the breakout of Allied forces from the Normandy beachhead in late July, airlift of supplies had not seemed urgent. The small airlift effort of August had been unimpressive. A shortage of airfields and trucks on the Continent curtailed operations. To restore captured airfields and to build new ones, some critical engineer materials had to be shipped by air. C-47s of IX Troop Carrier Command flew more than 5200 sorties during a 10-day period in early September. They carried over 15,000 tons of freight, including nearly 2,500,000 gallons of gasoline. This quantity of gasoline could meet the Third Army's needs for about three days.[1]

General Brereton, commander of FAAA, complained to Eisenhower that FAAA could not train personnel and execute combat operations if its transports were hauling supplies. Bradley and Montgomery urged the supreme commander to increase airlifts to ground forces. In their view, it was more important to supply 21st and 12th Army Groups than to execute airborne operations at a time when enemy forces were retreating.

Eisenhower felt pressure from the War Department to use his airborne forces aggressively. Arnold and Marshall wanted him to make "strategic" use of FAAA, that is, drop it into the German rear astride lines of communication, into an area with airfields that could be used to supply the force.[2]

Neither Eisenhower nor Bradley had much confidence in such a tactic. They considered it reckless. Bradley and Montgomery preferred to use airborne troops as infantry. Never a fan of Brereton's, Bradley wrote: "Almost from the day of its creation, this Allied Airborne Arm showed an astonishing faculty for devising missions that were never needed."[3]

With commendable adaptability, IX TCC switched to supply missions frequently in August and September, but airborne drops planned and later cancelled tied up transport aircraft. On August 29 SHAEF ordered Spaatz to convert 200 heavy bombers for use as transports. A few days later FAAA was ordered to use one-half of its transports to carry supplies to ground forces. Engineers laid pierced steel plank on the runways of several airstrips to handle heavily loaded aircraft.[4]

The C-47, a two-motored transport, could land on improvised runways without ground radio or beacon help. It could fly safely at speeds as slow as 110 miles per hour, a crucial characteristic for parachute operations. It was a forgiving aircraft to fly, well-constructed and readily maintained to give a very high rate of serviceability. Pilots sometimes landed C-47s on pastures after buzzing the fields to scare off grazing livestock. C-47s could carry 120 five-gallon jerricans of gasoline. Jerricans were sturdy and stackable. Airmen tied them securely to floor rings of C-47s.[5]

Heavy bomber groups were given little warning to be ready to carry gasoline. The change required extensive aircraft modification and crew training. Before gasoline could be carried safely, the weight of the bomber had to be reduced by removing ball turret, bombsight, armor plate ammunition, waist guns and loose equipment. Ground crews built wooden decks for bombers assigned to supply missions. They installed gasoline tanks in some bombers.

In September the Allied air forces had only a few airfields in France with runways long enough and strong enough to take the pounding given them by loaded B-24s. Between August 29 and September 17, those bombers of the Eighth Air Force assigned to supply missions carried food, gasoline and medical supplies to France.[6]

The 467th Bombardment Group executed supply missions on four-

teen days in September. It carried 646,079 gallons of gasoline to airfields in France. Each bomber was manned by a crew of five on supply missions.

Flights of five or six aircraft on supply runs might be escorted by fighters, but single transports often flew unescorted. Incredibly, in spite of ground fire, enemy fighters, rough runways, difficult navigation problems, and crew fatigue, the 81st Troop Carrier Squadron did not lose a single airplane on supply missions. Allied air supremacy helped these unarmed aircraft operate in relative safety.[7]

Loading and unloading cargoes several times delayed supply operations. Patton complained about employment of trained combat soldiers as truckers. Airmen had the same gripe. Often, air crews had to load and unload their aircraft. After unloading supplies, C-47s were often directed to other airstrips to pick up wounded soldiers to take to the U.K.

The total airlift to ground forces during September was close to 40,000 tons, almost a fourth of it by heavy bombers. The use of B-24s to carry supplies was highly uneconomical. It diverted them from their strategic targets. The Deputy Supreme Commander, Air Chief Marshal Tedder, recalled that "it was costing us one and a half gallons of 100-octane gasoline to deliver one gallon of 80-octane motor fuel to the forward depots."[8]

Lieutenant General James Doolittle, commander of the Eighth Air Force, wrote a letter to Spaatz, in his candid and logical manner, explaining the drawbacks of "our recent B-24 trucking operations":

> Bad weather and the diversion of the Eighth Air Force from strategic targets to direct support of ground forces has caused us to get far behind where we would like to be in our destruction of munitions in being and the German productive capacity for aircraft, oil, armament, tanks, motors, motor transport and other military equipment and supplies....
>
> There will be an even smaller percentage of days when weather conditions are good for strategic bombing as the winter season sets in.[9]

An AAF history records that the potential strength of air transport was never fully exploited in OVERLORD, "in large measure because of the failure to establish a single responsible air transport headquarters...."[10]

The following list shows amounts of supplies carried by the 438th Troop Carrier Group in September (in pounds):

Opposite: Soldiers unloading jerricans from a C-47 (courtesy of USAFHRA).

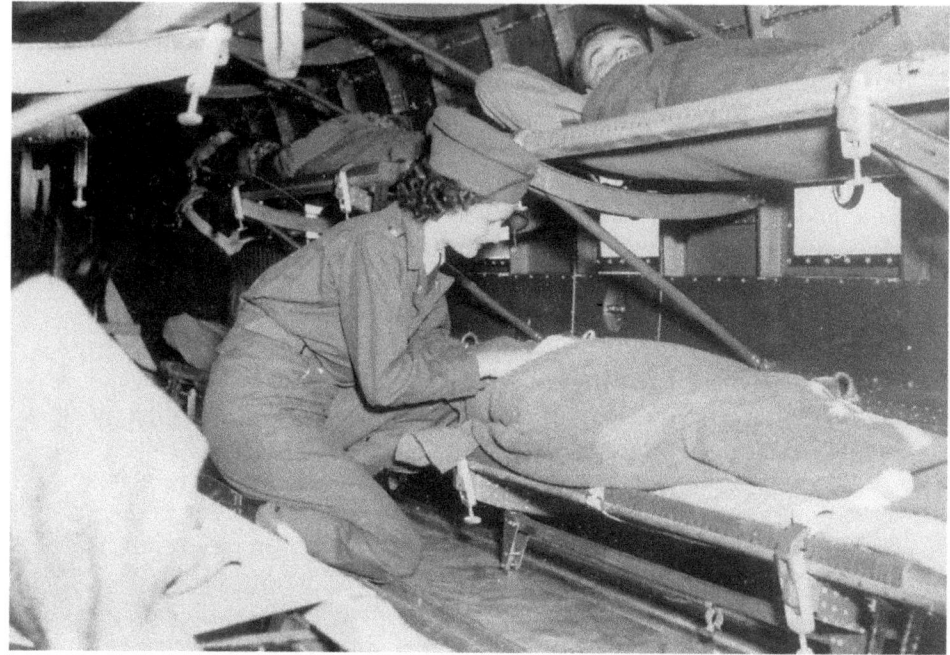

Nurse assisting a wounded soldier aboard a C-47 (courtesy of NARA).

Medical	35,564	Rations	622,285
Gasoline	2,911,209	Ammunition	371,873
Clothing	250,000	Ordnance	52,515
Signal	35,804	Misc.	169,512

The Group also evacuated 3290 medical patients.[11]

The normal supply requirements of one armored division was 415 tons per day. C-47s could carry this tonnage in 166 sorties. Heavy bombers required about 138 trips to carry the same amount.[12]

Weather and lack of airfields limited air supply. One landing strip could handle daily supplies for one armored division. In the area between Paris and the Rhine there were 11 airfields suitable for heavy bombers and 15 airfields suitable for troop carrier aircraft. Most of these needed rehabilitation to repair damage caused by bombing or demolitions.

Spaatz worried about a statement by Arnold that heavy bomber groups should soon be transferred to the Continent. He warned Arnold that such a move would complicate an already critical logistics situation:

10. Air Supply for Ground Forces

A. No air force is mobile without prepared bases.
B. There is a shortage now of Aviation Engineers and Signal construction units, reducing the potentiality of fighters, medium bombers and troop carriers....
C. The repair of railways is not keeping pace with the priority requirements of ground forces. This has forced the use of heavy bombers and troop carriers into carrying supplies....
D. The lack of railways is putting serious strain on motor transport.
E. There is serious doubt that ... port capacity would stand a traffic increase.[13]

The heavy bombers remained in England.

Despite their many weaknesses, Allied supply airlifts of August and September were significantly assisting ground forces when SHAEF ordered them cut sharply. Montgomery needed transport aircraft to carry airborne forces in a vital offensive in the north.

11

British Receive Priority for Supplies

The supply shortages that brought the Third Army to a five-day halt in September, and an even longer pause in October, were consequences of a general Allied logistics crisis. This unfortunate situation developed in part from misjudgments by SHAEF and COM Z. It was made more difficult to resolve by conflicts between Eisenhower and Montgomery.

In the three months after the landings in Normandy, Allied armies liberated most of France and were poised to invade Belgium, Luxembourg, Holland and Germany. OVERLORD vindicated the U.S. Army's doctrine that fast-moving armor, artillery and infantry with air support could defeat the formidable German military juggernaut. The Battle of France cost German forces about 500,000 soldiers and immense quantities of materiel. Overoptimistic rumors that forecast an early victory over Germany spread throughout Allied forces in September. Eisenhower's chief of intelligence predicted early in August that Germany would be defeated in three months.

Ironically, relations between Montgomery and Eisenhower worsened as Allied prospects improved. Tension between the two commanders increased in August after Marshall sent a curt message that Eisenhower must soon take direct command of Allied ground forces. This change, which Eisenhower planned to make on September 1, would reduce Montgomery's authority and would be seen as a downgrade to him. Americans, both military and civilian, did not want their forces commanded by foreign officers.

Montgomery urged Eisenhower not to take charge of ground operations. With much credibility, Montgomery argued that the supreme commander's responsibilities were so broad that he could not give the required attention to ground operations in addition to his many political, logistics and coordinating duties. Montgomery believed that SHAEF's staff was not competent to direct operations. Eisenhower was not swayed from his decision by Montgomery's appeals.

Appalled by the prospect of Eisenhower commanding ground forces directly, Montgomery made some proposals about strategy that would let him retain control over major Allied operations. He wanted full support for a powerful offensive in the north, to be directed by him. He asked the supreme commander to mass forty divisions for an offensive in the northeast to clear the Pas de Calais. The plan had some powerful reasons to support it:

1. Allied naval forces would protect the left flank of Montgomery's forces.
2. Channel ports would be captured.
3. It would liberate Belgium and the Netherlands.
4. Allied air forces based in the U.K. could support the offensive.
5. It would drive the Germans from rocket and flying-bomb launch sites.
6. It could lead to the capture of the Ruhr, Germany's industrial center.

Eisenhower agreed with most of Montgomery's proposal. He explained to Marshall: "Obviously we must drive hard to the northeast to complete the destruction of the principal concentration of enemy forces now in this region, seize the CROSSBOW [flying bomb and rocket launch] sites in the Pas de Calais area and the airfields in Western Belgium and then push on to secure a permanent and adequate base at Antwerp."[1]

Montgomery asked for support from the FAAA and the First Army to carry out this offensive. He advised the supreme commander to keep the Third Army in place and to allot it only a minimum of supplies until Allied forces in the north crossed the Rhine and opened up major ports such as Antwerp.

Eisenhower ordered the First Army to prepare to attack, in order to give support to the British offensive. He put the FAAA under Montgomery's authority.

Patton's supplies were cut sharply, but the Third Army continued to push eastward, supported by small amounts sent by COM Z and stocks captured from the Germans.

Eisenhower's assumption of direct control of Allied ground operations got off to a poor start. It coincided with an accident which put him in bed for days. He wrenched a knee trying to push a liaison plane back from the high water line on a beach near his headquarters at Granville.

On September 4 Eisenhower informed his subordinate commanders that the 21st Army Group had a mission to "secure Antwerp ... and then seize the Ruhr." The First Army would protect the flank of the 21st Army Group and "occupy the sector of the Seigfried line covering the Saar and then seize Frankfurt."[2]

Although Eisenhower agreed with Montgomery on many issues, they differed about the major goals of the British offensive in the North. The hottest point of disagreement concerned Montgomery's demand for a "powerful, full-blooded thrust to the Rhine and then Berlin." He wanted the Third Army to assume a "purely static role."

Eisenhower's reply to Montgomery explained that he favored offensives on a broad front. It was only the current logistics crisis that forced him to give a temporary priority to a drive in the north sector:

> While agreeing with your conception of a powerful and full blooded thrust towards the RUHR and Berlin, I do not agree that it should be initiated at this moment to the exclusion of all other maneuvers.... We must immediately exploit our success by promptly breaching the Siegfried Line, crossing the RHINE on a wide front, and seizing the SAAR and the RUHR.

Almost as an afterthought, Eisenhower wrote: "While we are advancing we will be opening the ports of Havre and Antwerp."[3]

In his personal journal, Eisenhower wrote: "From the beginning of this campaign I have always visualized that as soon as substantial destruction of the enemy force in France could be accomplished we should advance rapidly on the Rhine by pushing through the Aachen Gap in the north and through the Metz Gap in the south."[4] This statement, too, omits any mention of the crucial matter of ports. In the heady days of early September it seemed possible to "advance rapidly on the Rhine" without full logistics support.

Montgomery's proposal to execute a "full blooded, dagger thrust" into Germany provoked much ridicule at SHAEF. Eisenhower referred to a "pencil-like thrust," a proposal he called "fantastic." He believed such an effort would result in certain disaster. The debate that Eisenhower and Montgomery held on this question has continued endlessly. Eisenhower later defended his decision to push on a "broad Front," although he denied that he ever believed that Allied forces should be distributed in equal strengths along a front hundreds of miles long.

A U.S. Army history rejects the claims of Montgomery and Patton that their forces could have executed a successful invasion of Germany in 1944: "General Eisenhower's decision in mid-September was a decision based in large measure on logistic factors." Even if it had been possible to establish footholds in both the Saar and the Ruhr regions, "these areas were at the absolute maximum distance at which Allied forces could be supported for the time being; it would have been absolutely imperative to develop additional logistic capacity before attempting a power thrust deep into Germany."[5]

Montgomery continued to complain about lack of support. Eisenhower met with him on September 10 at an airfield near Brussels. Montgomery exuded confidence. The 21st Army Group had completed a rapid drive 280 miles east from the Seine. It seized excellent airfields and a railroad network in relatively sound condition. It was one of the most dramatic offensives of the war.

Montgomery described his plan for a bold but risky operation. He wanted FAAA to carry out an airborne drop deep in Holland. Parachute and glider troops would seize bridges along a 60-mile corridor leading to the Rhine near Arnhem. The British XXX Corps would race through the corridor to establish a bridgehead across the Rhine from which an invasion of the Ruhr could be launched.

Several influences weighed on the supreme commander to approve the proposal. He was reluctant to engage in another argument with Montgomery. He had received several strong suggestions from Arnold and Marshall to use his airborne forces more aggressively. He was influenced by optimistic reports that the Germans were too disorganized at the time to establish effective defenses. If successful, the operation would capture territory from which the Germans could launch rockets aimed at British cities. The most powerful influence was the need for ports on the coasts of Belgium and Holland. Historians later found it difficult to understand why he did not give Montgomery a clear order to open the port of Antwerp before attempting a drive toward Arnhem. Antwerp could not be used as a port until German positions along the Schelde estuary were eliminated.

On September 13 Eisenhower informed his chief subordinates of his goals: "...acquire some deep-water ports; push forward to the Rhine; clear the enemy from Brest; secure bridgeheads beyond the Moselle." The Third Army's advance through the Saar would take place after the Northern Group of Armies and First Army "have seized bridgeheads over the Rhine."[6]

On the same day, Eisenhower promised Montgomery that he would "make every effort to transport by motor truck to the Brussels area 500 tons of supplies per day. The motor transport required ... [will] be provided by immobilizing United States divisions ... and by employing every expedient. Naturally, such measures are emergency in character and must be temporary but I am prepared to put them into effect for a limited time to enable you to get across the Rhine and capture the approaches to Antwerp."[7]

Since D-Day, the FAAA had planned and cancelled eighteen operations. These aborted efforts involved tremendous waste. Bradley complained when aircraft ceased to bring supplies to the 12th Army Group, but Montgomery needed the transports for Operation MARKET-GARDEN, the drive toward Arnhem. Bradley found it hard to believe that Montgomery had proposed MARKET-GARDEN. "I would not have been more surprised," he wrote, "if Monty had come staggering, blind drunk, into my headquarters." Bradley saw clearly that MARKET-GARDEN required bold, aggressive command decisions of a kind that he had never associated with Montgomery.[8]

In a crucial part of the operation, the British XXX Corps would drive through a narrow corridor in enemy-held territory which had been seized by airborne troops. XXX Corps would link up with British airborne forces near Arnhem. American airborne soldiers would seize bridges which XXX Corps would use on its drive to Arnhem.

Operation MARKET, the airborne part of the offensive, began on Sunday morning, September 17. Air attacks on flak positions, artillery batteries, and radio and radar installations preceded the drops. A fleet of 1546 aircraft and 478 gliders brought airborne troopers to their assigned sectors in the best-executed Allied airborne operation of the war.[9]

German reaction to MARKET-GARDEN was prompt, strong and organized. Allied intelligence estimates had exaggerated enemy disorganization. Troops of the British 1st Airborne Division dropped into territory occupied by two panzer divisions, whose presence there had been largely undetected.

British paratroopers fought hard to capture a crucial bridge over the Neder Rijn but could not hold it against determined German attacks.[10]

Two American airborne divisions captured their objectives after heavy fighting. The 101st Division took Eindhoven on September 18; the 82nd Division captured Nijmegen on September 20. They seized important bridges and kept them open for the British XXX Corps, which was supposed to drive along the corridor to Arnhem.

Unfavorable weather after the first day reduced air support for MARKET-GARDEN. It was one of the causes for the failure to capture Arnhem. A more important cause was the slow progress of the British XXX Corps. This force never came close to linking up with the British forces at Arnhem. American airborne troops fought hard for days to repel German counterattacks on Allied lines of communication.

On September 25 the British 1st Airborne Division began to withdraw from the Arnhem area. Its tragic losses included 1485 men killed and 6525 missing.

American airborne divisions remained in combat in Holland until November, fighting as infantry to hold ground they had taken. This left them weakened at the start of the winter campaigns.

C-47 towing a glider (courtesy of NARA).

General Brereton recorded an accurate commendation about American airborne troops: "In the years to come everyone will remember Arnhem, but no one will remember that two American divisions fought their hearts out in the Dutch canal country and whipped hell out of the Germans."[11] The Americans achieved every objective assigned to them.

Brigadier General James M. Gavin, commander of the 82nd Airborne Division, parachuted into Holland during Operation MARKET. He called the performance of IX TCC "the best in the history of this Division. The accuracy, altitude and speed during drop were considered ideal by all participants.[12] Gavin's major criticism of IX TCC related to glider pilots who arrived unequipped and unorganized for ground fighting.

Not all participants in MARKET believed that the FAAA's performance had been exemplary. The commander of the British 1st Airborne Division complained that the drop zones for gliders were too far from Arnhem. The tactical air forces could also have done more, he believed: "Whatever the reasons, fighter support was not forthcoming except in small numbers and very late in the battle."[13]

General Spaatz reported to Arnold about AAF support for ground forces during MARKET-GARDEN. Eighth Air Force fighters "paid a price in men and airplanes [that] exceeds that of all other supporting Air Forces," he wrote. Spaatz reminded Arnold that the Eighth Air Force assigned "an entire B-24 wing to carry supplies to ground troops for six weeks while the Ninth Troop Carrier Command was occupied with airborne operations.... My personal feeling is that a major airborne operation is not generally justified in the immediate front of a rapidly moving situation. It is possible that the armies would have slowed down from lack of supplies anyway but the air lift which was denied them as a result of 'Market' and the several successive alerts which preceded it would have been considerable. There is no doubt that our logistics breakdown allowed the enemy to consolidate this side of the Rhine."[14]

On September 20 Eisenhower called Montgomery's attention to the need to clear the approaches to Antwerp. In this message Eisenhower wrote: "I cannot believe there is any great difference in our [strategic] concepts."[15]

Montgomery's reply had a peremptory tone: "I cannot agree that our concepts are the same.... I have always said stop the right and go on with the left, but the right has been allowed to go on so far that it has outstripped its maintenance and we have lost flexibility.... I would say that the right flank [Third Army] of 12 Army Group should be given very direct orders to halt...."[16]

The next day Montgomery sent a note to Eisenhower's chief of staff, Bedell-Smith: "...the tactical battle will require very tight control and very careful handling. I recommend that the Supreme Commander hands over the job to me, and gives me powers of operational control over First U.S. Army." [17]

At a meeting on September 22, which Montgomery refused to attend, Eisenhower made it clear that the possession of a major, deep-water port on the Channel was a prerequisite for the final drive into Germany.

With most Allied supplies coming through Cherbourg and over the Normandy beaches, and 150 freighters waiting to unload cargoes, Eisenhower was subjected to a storm of criticism about the delay in opening Antwerp.

As late as October 9, Montgomery had still not started a major push to clear Antwerp. Eisenhower sent a telegram to Montgomery: "Unless we have Antwerp producing by the middle of November our entire operations will come to a standstill.... I consider Antwerp of first importance, and I believe that the operations designed to clear up the entrance require your personal attention."[18] Another week passed before Montgomery gave unequivocal priority to Antwerp.

Montgomery continued to criticize Eisenhower. He circulated a paper,

Field Marshal B. L. Montgomery crossing the Seine River at Vernon (courtesy of the Imperial War Museum, BN552).

"Notes on Command in Western Europe." It charged that, "...we have 'mucked' the whole show and we have only ourselves to blame.... All our troubles can be traced to the fact that there is no one commander in charge of the land battle. The supreme commander runs it himself from SHAEF by means of long telegrams. SHAEF is not an operational headquarters and never can be."[19]

In letters to the British War Office, Montgomery expressed contempt for Eisenhower: "He has never commanded anything before in his whole career. Now, for the first time, he has elected to take direct command of very large-scale operations and he does not know how to do it."[20]

Montgomery's attitude and opinions were well-known at SHAEF. Eisenhower finally decided that the disagreements between himself and Montgomery could no longer be glossed over. He informed Montgomery that if they could not settle their differences, "it was our duty to refer the matter to higher authority for any action they may choose to take, however drastic."[21]

Montgomery replied on October 16: "You will hear no more on the subject of command from me. I have given you my views and you have given your answer.... I and all of us here will weigh in 100 per cent to do what you want and we will pull it through without a doubt. I have given Antwerp top priority in all operations of 21 Army Group and all our energies and efforts will be now devoted towards opening up that place." [22]

In accord with Hitler's strategy to deny ports to the Allies for as long as possible, the Germans had reinforced positions along the shores of the Schelde estuary. The Canadian First Army opened a campaign on October 1 to clear approaches to Antwerp. This goal was achieved on November 8. Allied ships began to unload cargoes at the port on November 28. Thereafter, the port handled a large share of OVERLORD's supplies.

The Canadian offensive to clear the approaches to Antwerp received strong support from Allied heavy bombers. Air Chief Marshal Harris complained: "Meanwhile the urgent necessity for preventing the enemy from firing guns at the First Canadian Army has taken an enormous proportion of effort...."[23]

During September, as SHAEF gave priority to operations on the north flank through the Pas de Calais and into Belgium and Holland, Third Army continued to push eastward despite occasional orders to halt offensive operations. There is no justification for the charge that Patton put Third Army into situations that risked its annihilation so that it would have to receive supplies. Some of his bombastic statements can be interpreted to indicate that he favored such recklessness but in reality he calculated risks accurately and believed that in a crisis he would be able to "pull something out of the hat."

12

The Drive to the Moselle

When the Third Army crossed the Seine southeast of Paris in the last days of August, it deployed two corps:

XII Corps	XX Corps
4th Armored Division	7th Armored Division
35th Infantry Division	5th Infantry Division
80th Infantry Division	90th Infantry Division

The Third Army also had
        8 squadrons of mechanized cavalry,
        23 antiaircraft battalions,
        20 combat engineer battalions,
        15 tank destroyer battalions,
        51 field artillery battalions,
        3 engineer general service regiments.

Tank destroyer battalions employed mobile guns capable of hitting enemy armor at ranges up to 2000 yards. They often provided mobile firepower in support of infantry. In a fierce battle near Metz they helped repel repeated German tank attacks.

XV Corps, part of the Third Army in August, was now assigned To the First Army. VIII Corps was a part of the Ninth Army.

Major General Manton Eddy replaced Cook as commander of XII Corps in August. Eddy had commanded a division in the Normandy battles. Eisenhower informed Marshall of the changes: "Major General Gilbert Cook, who has performed brilliantly as commander of XII Corps, has been relieved because of physical disability. His difficulty seems to result from an extraordinary high blood pressure...."[1]

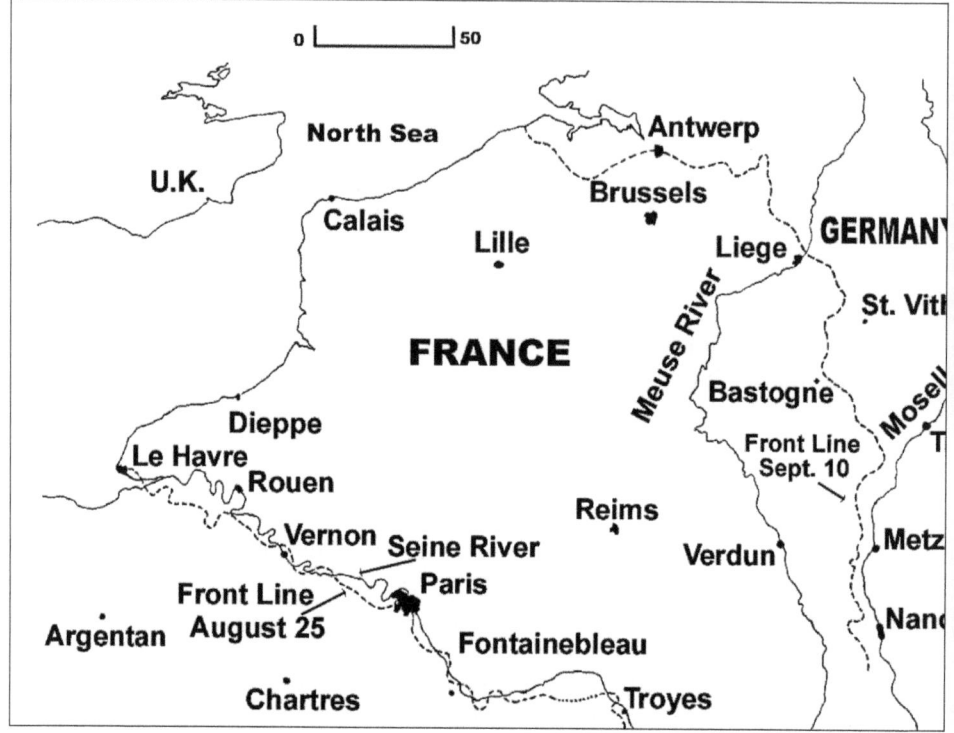

Map 5. Allied Front Lines, August and September 1944

In the closing days of August, both XII and XX Corps moved rapidly eastward against weak opposition. On August 28, the CCA of the 4th Armored Division raced fifty miles from Troyes to Vitry-le-François and crossed the Marne River. The next day the 4th Armored took Châlons-sur-Marne, where it captured more than 100,000 gallons of fuel. XII Corps continued its extraordinary progress on August 31 by taking Commercy, Joinville, Vaucouleurs and St. Mihiel. These actions gave it three bridgeheads over the Meuse River. In a lightning thrust, a battalion commanded by Lieut. Colonel Creighton Abrams attacked in a driving rain and captured a bridge across the Meuse at Commercy before the enemy could demolish it.[2] By September 1, XII Corps had almost exhausted its supply of gasoline.

XX Corps also made impressive progress. On August 26 the 5th Division took Nogent-sur-Seine. On August 30 it occupied Reims.

With help from the Resistance [FFI], the 7th Armored Division prevented demolition of a bridge across the Meuse River at Verdun. Tanks of the 7th Armored Division entered Verdun on September 1.

12. The Drive to the Moselle

In the final days of August, almost no gasoline arrived to replenish XX Corps' supplies. Its vehicles halted, with gasoline gauges on "empty." With their last gallons of gasoline, the 7th Armored and 5th Infantry Divisions crossed the Meuse River and established a bridgehead. A reconnaissance squadron scouted the area east of the Meuse to the Moselle River. It reported: "No enemy visible on other side of the Moselle. Many good places for bridges, all undefended."[3]

The gasoline drought continued during the first week of September. FFI informants reported that German troops were entering Metz and strengthening positions around this fortress city on the Moselle, which guarded a historic warpath between France and Germany.

The Third Army's advance across France exploited German disorganization. It was a motorized offensive. Soldiers rode on tanks, trucks, tank destroyers, armored personnel carriers and jeeps. Some moved in captured enemy vehicles. Patton urged subordinates to keep moving, despite open flanks, lack of control, bypassed enemy positions and other potential problems.

Many bonuses resulted from the speed of the Third Army's advance. German troops, many of them using horse-drawn wagons, bicycles, or on foot, had great difficulty establishing strong defensive positions or concealing themselves from fighter-bombers. The Third Army captured some useful supply dumps. Many bridges, airfields, communications systems, barges and boats were seized before they could be made inoperable by demolitions.

The 5th Division was proud of its mobility. It moved with the speed of an armored division. Its three regiments of infantry, with supporting artillery and armor, executed river crossings, assaulted strongpoints and established key bridgeheads.

Despite many victories, shortages frustrated Patton and his subordinates. Eddy recorded: "I am convinced that if we could obtain the necessary fuel the war might be over in a matter of a few weeks."[4] To conserve truck space for fuel, Army supply services delayed transport of such items as boots, clothing and blankets.

To strengthen his forces in the west in September, Hitler's police combed out men from the civilian population and rear echelon units and sent them to the western front. German women and workers from occupied countries kept the German war machine operating. Shorter lines of communication in the west were easier to maintain. The German armies' rear areas were now populated by friendlier people, with less activity by Resistance forces. Many experienced combat soldiers, who had avoided capture in France, now prepared to defend their fatherland. Pauses in

Allied offensive operations, caused by fuel shortages, gave German commanders time to establish strong defensive positions.

Not all the effects of pauses in offensive operations were negative to the Third Army. They gave troops some rest, and time to service, repair or replace equipment, and to train replacement personnel.

With both Allied and German forces moving steadily across France, XIX TAC put less emphasis on interdiction and more on armed reconnaissance. Fighter-bombers searched assigned areas for targets. Considerable time and gasoline were saved when pilots knew precisely where Allied units were located, but this was often difficult to determine. Fuel and truck shortages, and overcast weather conditions restricted air operations in September.

XIX TAC's 10th Photographic Reconnaissance Group made good use of clear days in September. It flew 822 visual and 314 photo recon sorties. It photographed fortifications around Metz, and the Siegfried Line, in addition to routine missions involving assessment of bomb damage.[5]

During the period of September 10 to 13, the 31st Photographic Reconnaissance Squadron photographed approximately 10,000 square miles of territory, and supplied more than 200,000 prints to the Third Army.[6]

A-20 pilots spotted a German column near the Loire on September 7. The 406th Fighter Group attacked it and destroyed 132 motor vehicles and 310 horse-drawn wagons. This fighter group destroyed 15 tanks near Nancy on September 10.

On one day in late September, XIX TAC flew 39 missions in which it destroyed or damaged 49 motor vehicles, two tanks, 67 locomotives, 371 railroad cars, a bridge, 18 gun positions, nine canal boats, 10 enemy buildings, two ammunition buildings, and 16 aircraft. It also spotted for artillery and dropped leaflets which advised German troops to surrender.[7]

The 405 Fighter Group moved to an airfield near St. Dizier in September. Explosives had been set to damage runways, but the Resistance cut the wires. The 405th received commendations for the support it gave XX Corps and XII Corps in battles along the Moselle.[8]

Fighter groups tried to keep close to ground forces. Between September 19 and 24, the 362nd Fighter Group moved from Brittany to Reims. Some men went by C-47, others by truck. A few officers used a captured wood-burning bus, which had to stop every few miles to refuel. They passed through a land beautiful in autumn, with fresh vegetables and fruit available. The Group's historian recorded: "As a sign of better times some equipment was also transported by rail."[9]

XIX TAC's interdiction campaign in the Loire region was curtailed when many of its groups were assigned to support the campaign to take

Brest. This reduction in reconnaissance and interdiction made it easier for many German soldiers to escape capture.

In mid–September an incident occurred which cheered the Ninth Air Force and demonstrated the value of its armed reconnaissance efforts. A force of 20,000 German troops, commanded by Major General Eric Elster, was spotted south of the Loire. Under continuous air attack in daylight, and harassed by the FFI, Elster notified the U.S. Ninth Army that he would surrender, provided air attacks ceased and his troops were not handed over to the French. The Ninth Army commander invited Weyland to attend the surrender ceremonies near Orléans. "Inasmuch as your command has been instrumental in accomplishing this surrender, request that you or your representative be present ... to accept the surrender."[10]

With some Third Army units across the Moselle, XIX TAC supported ground forces more than 400 miles apart. The famous 354th Fighter Group had one of its memorable days on September 12. Its P-51 Mustangs shot down thirty-five aircraft in a 15-minute battle in the Frankfurt area. Pilots of the 354th Group reported that enemy pilots lacked competence.[11] Critical fuel shortages handicapped the Luftwaffe. Allied heavy bombers hit German oil refineries frequently. The resulting gasoline shortages made it necessary to reduce pilot-training flights.

Soon after Eisenhower assumed direct control of ground operations, he issued a long-range directive for the Third Army. It would push through the Siegfried Line, occupy the Saar, and seize Frankfurt. The message had somewhat conflicting elements: "It is important that this operation should start as soon as possible in order to forestall the enemy in this sector, but troops ... operating against the Ruhr northwest of the Ardennes must first be adequately supported."[12]

Hitler took another action to strengthen his forces in the west in early September. He appointed Field Marshal Gerd von Rundsted to command German armies there. Von Rundsted was instructed to cut off Allied armored spearheads, hold Belgium and the Netherlands north of the Schelde, and counterattack toward Reims.

Von Rundstedt soon made his influence felt. He ordered the Fifteenth Army to move across the Scheldt estuary. Approximately 65,000 troops, artillery, trucks and wagons were ferried from France to Holland, despite Allied air, land and sea superiority.[13]

Patton ordered XII and XX Corps to continue moving to the east whenever fuel became available. He expected only weak enemy resistance at the Moselle. Eddy favored a rapid drive to the Moselle before enemy defenses stiffened.

After XII Corps captured some German gasoline, and some more arrived through Army supply channels, Eddy sent a task force of the 80th Division to establish a bridgehead across the Moselle at Pont-à-Mousson, 15 miles north of Nancy. On the morning of September 5 this force tried to cross the river at a ford but was hit by devastating artillery fire. Some troops attempted to cross in assault boats but were repelled by machine gun and mortar fire. Other attacks during the evening and night met a similar fate. One battalion put four platoons across the river, but a German bayonet assault wiped out the position. Eddy ordered the 80th Division to postpone river crossings.

Walker's field order of September 5 reflected the optimism that pervaded Allied ranks. It forecast that XX Corps would advance rapidly to the Rhine at Mainz. With the 7th Armored Division in the lead, followed by the 90th and 5th Infantry Divisions, XX Corps moved toward the Moselle on September 7. Thionville was the 90th Division's objective. The 5th Division moved toward Metz.

The 7th Armored received orders to cross the Moselle, bypass Metz and drive for the Sarre River. It was the kind of cavalry maneuver that Patton and Walker favored. The German front that XX Corps intended to roll up was some eighteen miles west of Metz and the Moselle. There are major rivers in the area. East of the Moselle there is a high, rugged plateau, with dense woods and many deep ravines. It is difficult for tanks to maneuver in this kind of terrain.

Patton's estimate of German intentions was inaccurate. They planned to fight hard to hold a line at the Moselle.

The 7th Armored Division, commanded by Major General Lindsay Silvester, was a well-trained division with high morale. Soon after it joined XX Corps on August 14, Patton told Silvester that he "was not satisfied with his division, either as to looks or progress, and that he had to do better at once."[14] The division did well in its march across France. It participated in the capture of Chartres, Melun and Dreux. It was one of the first units to cross the Seine. In a 3-week drive the 7th Armored traveled 600 miles and helped liberate some 150 French towns, including Reims and Verdun.

For six days the 7th Armored remained in Verdun waiting for fuel. When it attempted to seize crossings over the Moselle near Metz, it ran into heavy artillery fire, and several of its columns had to halt short of the river.

Patton asked Bradley for orders to move two divisions eastward "…and let the Loire take care of itself. No supply line runs near it and the enemy who is fool enough to cross it would have to walk. As it is we have two divisions guarding nothing…. But Bradley said, 'I can't take the risk.' And by so saying takes a much worse risk [failing to exploit opportunities]."[15]

12. The Drive to the Moselle 127

5th Division soldiers crossing the Moselle (courtesy of USAMHI).

The 5th Division tried to cross the Moselle near Dornot but came under heavy artillery fire from Fort Driant on high ground to the north. A few infantry companies made it across the river but were surrounded by panzer forces. Accurate artillery fire caused heavy losses in the American units.

The Dornot bridgehead was abandoned and the surviving troops moved back across the Moselle. Some soldiers crossed the river by swimming, and some drowned in the turbulent river. Units of the 5th Division in the bridgehead at Dornot repelled more than thirty assaults.[16]

At 0200 on September 10, the 10th Regiment of the 5th Division crossed the Moselle near Arnaville in assault boats. Heavy fighting took place to hold this bridgehead eight miles southwest of Metz. German infantry and tanks attacked the American force, and it was hit by artillery from forts in the area.

The 5th Division expanded the Arnaville bridgehead slowly, with its troops under heavy artillery fire. Supplies had to be ferried over the river, which was high and swift from heavy rainfall. Engineers struggled to construct a bridge, but rapid currents and accurate artillery slowed the effort. Smoke generators helped conceal bridge construction and supply

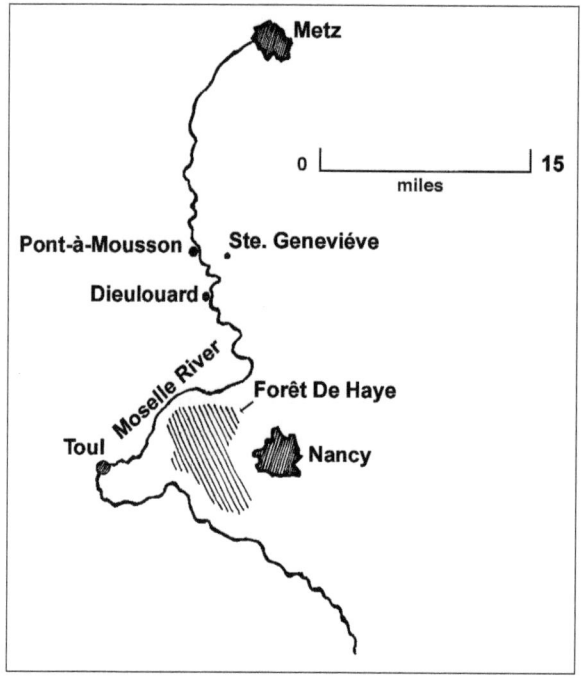

Map 6. Nancy Area

boats. Liaison aircraft checked to see if the smoke was doing its job of concealment.

XIX TAC took advantage of clear skies on September 12. P-47s of the 406th Fighter Group helped repel an attack by infantry, tanks and assault guns. The 5th Division's commander recorded that air support was "splendid and has been of the greatest value. It [XIX TAC] operates quickly and efficiently, and has uncanny ability to find targets...."[17]

During the next two months the Ninth Air Force supported third Army operations in the Moselle region whenever weather permitted effective air operations. Much of the fighter-bomber effort directed at Metz forts was wasted. Bombs less than 2000 pounds did little damage to forts. P-47s usually carried bombs weighing 500 or 1000 pounds.[18]

Engineers completed a bridge across the Moselle on September 12. Tanks of the 7th Armored crossed the river to reinforce the bridgehead near Arnaville.

XII Corps also encountered strong enemy resistance as it tried to establish a bridgehead near Nancy. On September 11 Eddy sent the 35th Infantry and 4th Armored Divisions on a wide arc across the Moselle to attack Nancy from the east, with strong support from air and artillery units. North of Nancy, CCA of the 4th Armored Division and the 80th Infantry Division crossed the Moselle on September 11–12. Heavy fighting continued for three days as German counter-attacks tried to push the 80th Division back to the river. The CCA crossed the river on a treadway bridge and helped break up German attacks. The 80th Division held its ground, with heavy losses on both sides.

The CCA drove the enemy from Ste. Geneviéve and wheeled to the southeast. It crashed through enemy road blocks, captured 354 prisoners, destroyed 12 tanks, and killed or wounded a considerable number of the enemy.

The French Resistance reported on September 14 that the Germans were evacuating Nancy. The CCA received orders to cut highways east of the city. It knifed through a panzer grenadier division at Arracourt and spent a week behind enemy lines.

In fog and rain on September 19, the 4th Armored Division engaged enemy panzer forces near Arracourt in a battle that lasted for three days. The 4th Armored destroyed 43 German tanks. It lost five medium tanks and three tank destroyers.

In battles near Arracourt, tank destroyers helped repel repeated German attacks. A commander of a tank destroyer platoon claimed that his unit destroyed 15 tanks.[19]

On September 24 a volksgrenadier division and a panzer brigade attacked the 4th Armored Division west of Château Salins. At 1000, fighter-bombers of XIX TAC struck the German armor and helped repel the attackers.

In little more than a month, the 4th Armored Division had advanced seven hundred miles and crossed three major rivers. Since crossing the Moselle it had destroyed or damaged an estimated 285 German armored vehicles. One of its battalion commanders recorded: "The German border lay a scant seventy miles away, a day's march for armor."[20]

The Forêt de Haye, west of Nancy, worried Eddy. "Nobody knows what is in there," he told Vandenberg. IX Bomber Command sent seven groups of medium bombers to bomb the forest.[21]

Patton instructed his corps commanders to hold adequate bridgeheads across the Moselle, but his major goals lie to the east beyond the German frontier. He planned to send the Third Army toward the Rhine. His

	Armor		Armament
	Front	Side	Cannon
German Tiger Mark I	100 mm	80 mm	88 mm
German Tiger Mark II	150 mm	100 mm	88 mm
German Panther	100 mm	45 mm	75 mm
U.S. Sherman	75mm	51 mm	75 mm

The Panther, with a higher muzzle velocity, outgunned the Sherman. A later model of the Sherman had a 76 mm gun with a higher muzzle velocity.

Table 5. Tank Characteristics

staff was working on plans which would send XX Corps to take Frankfurt, XII Corps to capture Darmstadt, and XV Corps (again a part of the Third Army) to Mannheim.

German opposition in the Moselle area remained tough. Positions were defended with tenacity, and counterattacks slowed American progress.

Fighter-bombers of XIX TAC, and artillery of the 4th Armored helped repel an attack by infantry and 30 tanks on September 24. German casualties were 300 killed, 500 wounded, and 194 captured. They lost 21 tanks.

The 405th Fighter Group received a Distinguished Unit Citation for actions in this tank battle. On an overcast day, its pilots repeatedly flew as low as 800 feet to break up a panzer force.[22]

Tank battles near the Moselle in September demonstrated the weaknesses and strengths of American armor. During training in the U.S. and U.K., American tank crews were told that their equipment was equivalent to German armor. This belief was shattered in France. American tanks were inferior to German tanks in firepower, armor and mobility in mud. U.S. tank losses were high, although efficient ordnance recovery teams retrieved tanks which could be salvaged.[23]

The U.S. M-4 Sherman medium tank had a 75 mm gun (muzzle velocity of 2050 feet per second), and two .30 caliber and one .50 caliber machine guns. Some Allied tanks were modified to serve as flamethrowers and to clear mine fields. American tanks were faster on paved roads, but they tended to flounder in muddy terrain. Tank crews and ordnance specialists improvised various devices to improve traction.

When tanks were hit, the entire crew often became casualties. Incendiary shells set gasoline and ammunition ablaze. A serious shortage of tank crews developed in American armored units.[24]

Many tank maintenance soldiers came from farms. They were experienced in working with machinery and often devised mechanical improvements on equipment. Many of them had received special training in ordnance.

The shortage of railroads hurt Allied armored divisions. If tanks were brought to the front under their own power the trips reduced the time their engines and tracks could operate in combat without overhaul.

When it entered combat in France, the 4th Armored Division's tanks were manned by well-trained crews with a high level of competence. Many months of training paid off. A powered traversing turret compensated for the Sherman's smaller gun. Gunners fired quickly, and aimed at the rear and tracks of enemy tanks. So did fighter-bombers. American tankers fired accurately while in motion, something Germans rarely did.[25]

12. The Drive to the Moselle

In the center of XX Corps' front, the 5th Infantry division pushed toward Metz, one of the most heavily fortified regions in the world. Armies had fought for this area for thousands of years. In spite of Metz's long martial history, XX Corps lacked accurate information about it. Germans had occupied the area for more than four years. The Ninth Air Force photographed the city and forts around it, but prints showed only superficial aspects. The city and its network of forts had such strong bastions that even mediocre garrisons could make attackers pay dearly. A U.S. Army history describes the German units in front of XX Corps:

> "...one demoralized and burned-out division, one untried and incomplete volksgrenadier division, one battle-weary SS division — lacking most of its tanks and assault guns but still possessed of good morale — one scratch division of heterogeneous units varying from very poor fortress troops to the trained and determined men from Metz [military] schools, and one panzer brigade whose potential strength was hardly that of an American armored combat command."[26]

Metz forts had received little improvement since World War I, and some had only small garrisons. However, their artillery could be devastating. They occupied high ground, and the guns of each fort could help defend nearby forts.

Patton's decision to attack Metz forts in September is puzzling. The Third Army was not supposed to be executing offensive operations. In his postwar book, Bradley called the Metz attacks an "unauthorized pecking campaign." He appealed to Patton to stop them: "For God's sake, George, lay off.... When we get going again, you can far more easily pinch out Metz and take it from behind."[27] Patton did not agree, and Bradley did not feel it would be appropriate to order an Army commander to halt minor attacks.

An attack by a regiment of the 5th Infantry Division west of Metz ran into stiff opposition. When the 7th Armored tried to support it on September 9, German artillery, with clear fields of fire, knocked out seven tanks. The 5th Division attacked Fort Driant. This fort had 100 mm and 150 mm guns protected by reinforced concrete casements. The battle seesawed for days, with heavy losses for the 5th Division. Eddy called off the attack.

The 90th Infantry Division on the left of XX Corps' front moved toward Thionville, a city on the Moselle north of Metz. A counterattack was beaten off on September 8, with German losses of thirty tanks, sixty half-tracks and many other vehicles. After days of heavy fighting, the 90th Division held almost all of Thionville west of the river.[28]

By mid–September, 5th Infantry Division troops were tired. They had suffered heavy losses attacking positions so strong they could withstand air and artillery bombardment. Moreover, XX Corps was short of artillery shells.

Walker was reluctant to curtail offensive operations, despite setbacks and the pessimism of some of his subordinates. On September 14 he ordered the 7th Armored to attack through the 5th Division's bridgehead near Arnaville. It would drive around Metz and threaten German positions north of the city. The offensive would be supported by a 5th Division attack to enlarge its bridgehead. The plan involved complex maneuvers with exceptional risks.

The 7th Armored encountered stiff opposition, especially from artillery. Instead of executing a free-wheeling march behind the enemy's front, the 7th Armored became bogged down in a battle for Sillegny, a town on the Seille River a few miles south of Metz. On the left, the 5th Division attempted to seize two small towns. In a battle for one of these towns, Pournoy-la-Chétive, fierce fighting continued for days; brutal and costly, it was "among the most bitterly fought actions in the Lorraine Campaign," an Army history records.[29]

On September 23, the 7th Armored Division was transferred to the First Army. The transfer consumed vast amounts of gasoline and truck space. It shortened the lives of tank engines and tracks. It crimped XX Corps' plans to attack. The 5th Division pulled back from positions it had fought hard for to cover an area left by the 7th Armored Division.

When the Third Army fought for bridgeheads on the Moselle, its right flank extended almost 500 miles—from St. Nazaire on the Bay of Biscay to Nancy. Much of it was guarded by small Third Army detachments, XIX TAC's fighter and reconnaissance aircraft, and the French Resistance. To Bradley the Loire flank was a nagging worry. It could not be extended much more without inviting attacks on it. On September 8 Patton assigned XV Corps to protect it. XV Corps now consisted of the 2nd French Armored Division (released from duties in Paris) and the 79th Infantry Division. Within a few days Patton found other tasks for XV Corps to supplement its flank-guarding. He ordered Haislip to send some units toward the Moselle.

At dawn on September 13 the 2nd French Armored Division encountered some Panther tanks near Dompaire, 40 miles south of Nancy and 10 miles west of the Moselle. The 406th Fighter Group hit the force four times with bombs and rockets. Sixty German tanks were destroyed. Later in the day the Germans left Dompaire.[30]

At Charmes, on the Moselle 20 miles south of Nancy, a regiment of the 79th Division forded the river, cleared the town, and secured a bridgehead on the east shore.

Patton met with Haislip on the afternoon of September 18 and ordered XV Corps to attack east of the Moselle. Haislip sent elements of the 79th Division to clear Lunéville and nearby forests in an area about 15 miles southeast of Nancy.

In and around the Forêt de Mondon, southeast of Lunéville, the 79th Division fought hand-to-hand battles, which drove enemy troops from the forest but cost the Americans nearly 200 casualties. The 2nd French Armored Division crossed the Meurth River during the night of September 22–23 and advanced along the southern part of the Forêt de Mondan until stopped by a panzer grenadier division.

Nancy was not a fortified city. After the Ninth Air Force bombed the Forêt de Haye on September 14, the FFI reported that the Germans were evacuating the city. The next day the 80th Infantry Division occupied Nancy with little opposition.

German forces in the Forêt de Grémecey posed a threat to XII Corps' use of a major highway east of Nancy. Eddy sent elements of the 6th Armored Division to occupy portions of the forest on September 22.

On September 25 the 35th Division began to relieve the 6th Armored in the Forêt de Grémecey when it was hit by strong enemy counterattacks. Heavy fighting went on for days within the forest and on its perimeter. When fog lifted on September 29, XIX TAC's fighter-bombers attacked German armor and infantry. In a commendation of the 405th Fighter Group, Weyland wrote: "One squadron dropped 16 500-pound bombs squarely in the center of a troop concentration.... Another squadron broke up a tank force east of Lunéville." The 405th Group destroyed 11 tanks during this mission.[31]

After listening to reports from regimental commanders, on September 30 Eddy ordered the 35th Division to withdraw. When Patton heard of this order he flew to XII Corps' headquarters and told Eddy to "hang on." Eddy ordered the 6th Armored Division to counterattack.[32] The 35th Division stiffened and held its positions. The 6th Armored attacked along the southern edge of the forest and seized the town of Chambrey, which it held throughout the day, despite constant shelling and many counterattacks. Inside the forest, Americans advanced against stubborn resistance. The Germans withdrew during the night of October 1–2. On October 2 fighter-bombers helped disperse enemy forces north of Chambrey.

In late September Patton ordered the Third Army to assume a defensive status, but not to "dig in, wire or mine." He wanted to conceal "the change in attitude" from the enemy.[33]

Patton complained about the iron grip of logistics on operations in September:

> I presented my case for a rapid advance to the east for the purpose of cutting the Siegfried Line before it could be manned. Bradley was very sympathetic; but, I gather, SHAEF's staff did not concur. It was my opinion then that this was the momentous error of the war. So far as the Third Army was concerned, we not only failed to get back gas due us, but got practically no more, because in consonance with the decision to move north, in which two corps of the First Army also participated, all supplies—both gasoline and ammunition—had to be thrown in that direction.... I was sure it was a horrible mistake to halt even at the Meuse, because we could continue to the Rhine.... I was convinced, and have since discovered that I was right, that there were no Germans ahead of us except those we were actually fighting.[34]

In September, supplies poured through Mediterranean Ports, but SHAEF sent few of them to the Third Army. Eisenhower decided to give full support to the 6th Army Group on the right flank of Allied forces.

The Ninth Air Force put less priority on close air support in late September and more on interdiction. On September 28 the 405th Fighter Group blew up two ammunition trains east of Nancy, one of which carried Tiger tanks.[35]

Two major facts support Patton's and Montgomery's proposals for September drives into Germany to establish bridgeheads from which to launch future offensives:

1. The best season for military operations in Europe was slipping away, and the worst one would begin in October. Clouds, rain, cold, ice, mud, and snow would handicap all Allied arms, but would hit armor and air forces particularly hard.
2. An Allied pause in offensive operations would give the Germans a respite during which they could strengthen their defenses in the west, which were disorganized and weak in September.

A high-ranking German officer agreed with Patton: "Had the Allies kept up the attack ... they could have pursued German forces until they dropped from exhaustion and could have ended the war half a year earlier."[36]

The pause in operations by the Third Army in October forced the Ninth Air Force to realign its Groups and change its priorities with regard to air support for American ground forces.

13

Air Support for the Third Army's Autumn Operations

After the campaign to capture Brest ended, the Ninth Air Force paid more attention to the Third Army's drive to the east. Fighter-bombers and medium bombers gave less close support to ground troops in the relatively static situation, but hit interdiction targets often.

By autumn, IX Engineer Command had provided a surplus of airfields from which aircraft operated to support the Third Army. On September 7 the 826th Aviation Engineer Battalion started to rehabilitate an airfield at St. Dizier. The next day work began on sod airstrips at Perthes, Orconte, and Vitry. An airstrip near St. Liviere became operational for supply and evacuation on September 12. Two sod fields near Reims served fighter-bombers.[1]

After transfers of fighter groups to other tactical air commands, the strength of XIX TAC in October was as follows: 354th, 358th, 362nd, 405th, 406th Fighter Groups; 10th Photographic Reconnaissance Group; and the 425th Night Fighter Squadron. The 405th Fighter Group and IX Bomber Command attacked Fort Driant on October 3. On October 8 the Group attacked a panzer force threatening XII Corps east of Nancy. The 358th Fighter Group dropped 25 tanks of napalm on three Metz forts. XIX TAC helped break up several armored counter-attacks in the Moselle region.

The prohibition against air attacks on railroad bridges was lifted in October. Bad weather made it difficult to monitor bomb damage on bridges and other targets. The Ninth Air Force attacked 33 bridges in October and destroyed 17. Taking advantage of cloudy days, when workers were not interrupted by air attacks, Germans repaired railroad lines, bridges and yards quickly.

On October 11, P-51 Mustangs of the 354th Fighter Group helped direct artillery fire at long-range, 280 mm guns in Metz. This group hit a

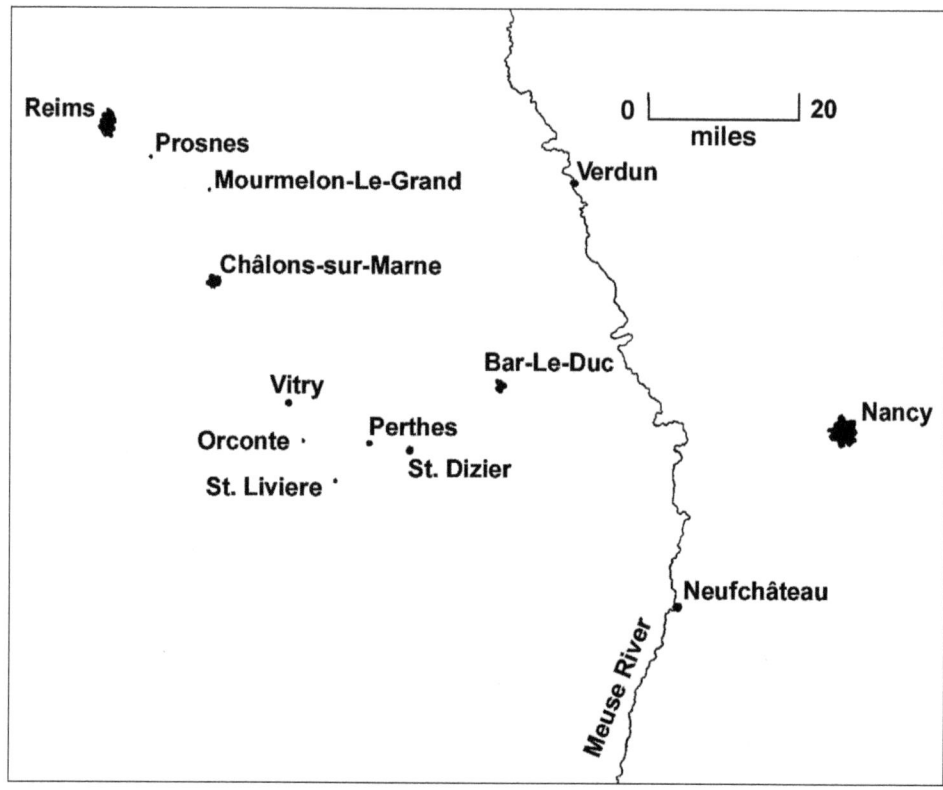

Map 7. Airfields West of the Third Army, September 1944

30-car ammunition train on October 12 in the Saar and blew it to pieces with machine-gun fire.[2]

The 362nd Fighter Group flew missions on 20 days of October, often through rain and overcast skies. On some missions it hit targets in the Saar, including locomotives, box cars, railroad yards and bridges. One of the Group's squadrons was trained and equipped to fire rockets. Rockets carried a large explosive charge at high speed and exerted little recoil on the aircraft that launched them.

October 8 was a banner day for the 362nd Group. It attacked airfields in Germany and destroyed 15 aircraft on the ground. On this same day it destroyed six locks on a canal east of Sarrebourg. The group hit a railroad bridge at Trier with nine 1000-pound bombs on October 13.[3]

During the hectic dash across France, XIX TAC's and Third Army's headquarters were often far apart. In October they occupied sites near each other in Nancy.

Allied tactical air force personnel felt an acute sense of frustration about their ineffectiveness at night and during overcast days. The 425th Night Fighter Squadron joined XIX TAC and began night operations on October 18. It flew P-61 aircraft and some worn-out A-20s. It attacked large transportation targets such as railroad marshalling yards. By use of wing racks, bomb loads of A-20s had been increased from 2000 to 3000 pounds without any significant loss of speed or maneuverability.

During good weather on October 20, XIX TAC launched 245 sorties. The 358th Fighter Group bombed and strafed rail yards near Koblenz at the confluence of the Moselle and Rhine rivers.

The 405th Fighter Group received a Presidential Unit Citation for its achievements in September. Its exceptional record was compiled in spite of a move from the Le Mans area to St. Dizier near the Marne River. The Group's history describes the move as "tumultuous." The weather was "distinguished only by leaden skies, cold damp days, rain and ubiquitous mud." All quartermaster trucks had been commandeered to supply ground forces. Nevertheless, the Group destroyed a substantial number of targets in October:[4]

Enemy aircraft	4	Military vehicles	123
Armored vehicles	5	Locomotives	111
Railroad cars	82	Bridges	4
Gun emplacements	36	Supply dumps	1
Factories	28	Road hubs	8
Railroad tracks	5	Boats, barges	24
Horse-drawn wagons	26	Marshalling yards	18
Airfields	1	Troop concentrations	16

The 406th Fighter Group executed a substantial number of ground support missions in September. Late in the month, the Group moved to an airfield near Mourmelon-le-Grand. Formerly, a French cavalry unit had occupied the site. The accommodations were excellent, with heated brick buildings. Officers organized a club with a swimming pool for themselves. On October 20 the Group blasted a train of 50 flat cars loaded with tanks, guns and motor vehicles.[5]

Cold, wet weather reminded Allied supply services to deliver winter clothing to soldiers and airmen. Eighth Air Force B-24s brought overcoats and boots with loads of gasoline. The 435th Troop Carrier Group hauled 3,121,839 pounds of clothing, rations and gasoline to Allied troops in October. It brought 1623 wounded soldiers to England.[6]

Anticipating greater need to operate in darkness and on overcast days, Weyland asked Vandenberg to retrieve radar equipment that had been borrowed by the Royal Air Force to help it defend England against flying bombs and rockets. The Allies used a vast amount of equipment in their efforts against these German V-weapons, including radar equipment, fighter aircraft, antiaircraft guns and shells, reconnaissance and intelligence resources, and medium and heavy bombers. A British historian called the Allied campaign against V-weapons "illogical and extravagant to an almost incredible degree."[7] It diverted resources from critical air and ground campaigns.

In October, the 10th Photographic Reconnaissance Group provided the Third Army with large-scale photo prints of forts, obstacles, roads, artillery positions, supply dumps, command centers, bridges and railroad yards in the Moselle and Saar regions.

The transfer of some of its groups to other tactical air commands, and bad weather, caused XIX TAC's sortie total to plummet from 12,292 in August to 3,509 in November.[8]

Bitter fighting along the Moselle in October created an urgent need for airstrips to evacuate wounded soldiers. To cope with the water-soaked clay of the Moselle region, engineers searched for materials to strengthen airfield surfaces. One battalion hauled slag from nearby smelters to finish off runways. Almost continuous maintenance of airfield access roads became necessary. Square mesh track runway surfacing material was not adequate in muddy conditions. Prefabricated hessian surfacing, a material made of jute impregnated with asphalt, was not much better in the miserable weather conditions of fall and winter. Pierced steel plank served well if the underlying surface was firm, but its heavy weight put a drain on transportation.[9]

A radar expert from the War Department visited the Ninth Air Force in October. He reported: "The tactical airforce is being forged into a real instrument for close cooperation with the armies." He rated armored column cover first in importance. Interdiction of railroads, destruction of bridges and general attack on road traffic came second. Reconnaissance provided the ground forces with "an astonishingly large section of their intelligence on the deployment and movement of enemy ground forces."[10]

In bad weather, radar helped pilots in many ways. When unable to find targets or their airfields, they called on radar operators for directions. Radar gave clues to judge whether pilots navigated accurately to target areas, made contact with friendly ground forces, and identified targets. Often, pilots needed radar help with at least one of these tasks.

The radar equipment available to the Ninth Air Force could handle only one mission every forty or fifty minutes. It did not have a capability to direct precision bombing. It could guide aircraft at night only to large targets, such as marshalling yards or towns.[11]

13. Air Support for the Third Army's Autumn Operations

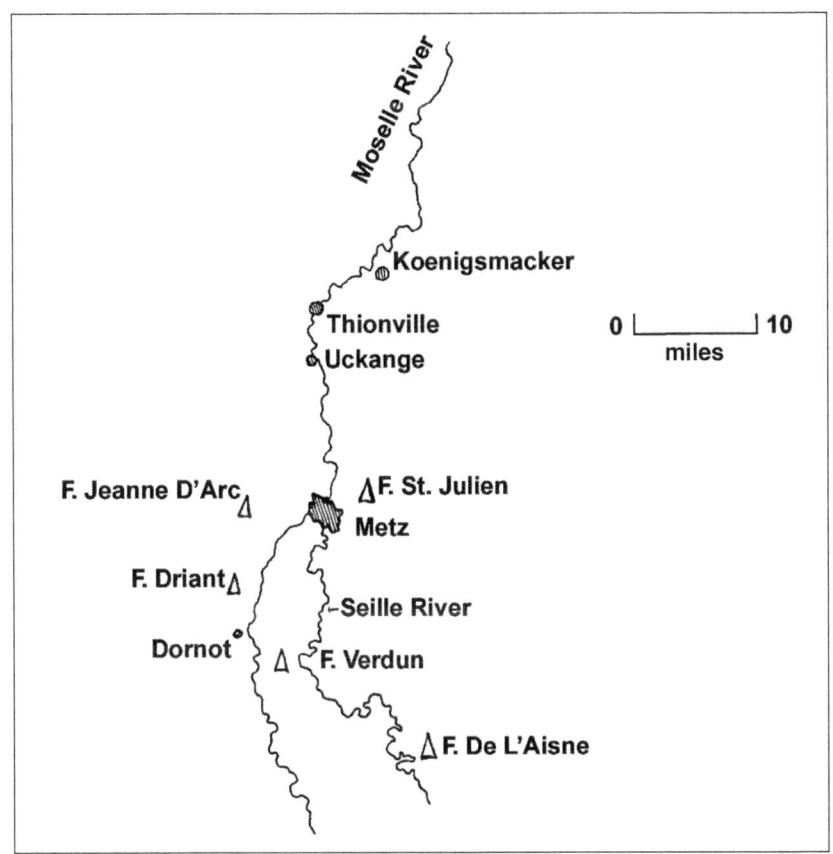

Map 8. Metz Area

Air attacks on fortifications such as those at Brest or Metz usually did little damage. Nevertheless, ground commanders repeatedly asked for air support, and airmen did not always reject such requests, even when they had sound reasons for doing so. XIX TAC struck Fort Driant daily from September 26 to 30 with little effect on its stone and concrete casemates seven feet thick. Fort Driant, overlooking the Moselle, occupied a dominant height from which artillery could be directed on targets in a large area.

Fifteen forts in an inner ring around Metz served primarily as infantry strongholds. Twenty-eight forts in an outer ring could fire large-caliber artillery weapons from guns protected by massive concrete casemates.

A witness to the attacks on Metz forts wrote: "We were pulled out from our position south of Thionville and thrown into futile and suicidal attacks on the great forts of Metz.... The poor infantrymen lying out there, soaking wet, covered with mud, and under murderous fire from the forts, were really taking it again.... All we had to do was to cross a mile-wide, muddy, soaked field swept by machine gun and artillery fire, traverse a deep moat filled with barbed wire, scale the walls on the other side and then assault a series of huge concrete fortresses built into a hill."[12]

After weeks of effort the situation at Fort Driant was near chaos. An officer with the assault force reported that, "enemy [artillery] is butchering these trs [troops] until we have nothing left to hold with. We cannot get out our wounded and there is a hell of a lot of dead and missing."[13] Walker decided to abandon the assault on October 9. It had taught the Third Army that troops needed better training and equipment to assault fortresses, that air attacks had limited value, and that it was often preferable to bypass forts and wait for their garrisons to surrender.

One of the "local actions" ordered by Patton sent the 90th Infantry Division to take Maizieres-les-Metz, a town a few miles north of Metz. It lay astride an important road. At 0430 on October 3, a regiment surprised the Germans in the town and took control of a slag pile. When the attack continued a few days later, Americans occupied the northern part of the village. Bitter house-to-house fighting went on for more than three weeks. Mines, booby traps, grenades, automatic weapons, mortars and artillery made German positions formidable. The 90th Infantry Division suffered 552 casualties in the battle, including 51 dead.[14]

German artillery, firing huge shells from guns placed on railroad cars, were a serious menace to Third Army units units. P-47s of XIX TAC silenced one battery by skip-bombing each end of a tunnel in which it sheltered when not firing.

XX Corps executed a successful counter-battery action against a 280 mm railroad gun in October. Information about its location came from aerial photographs, the French Resistance, and railroad workers. Intelligence personnel concluded that the gun was in a shed in a rail yard in Metz. XX Corps fired 140 rounds at the target, with help from XIX TAC's 12th Tactical Reconnaissance Squadron. The position was demolished.[15]

On October 11 the Third Army ceased direct assaults on fortified positions around Metz. Losses had been high, results meager, and illnesses spread among troops exposed to cold and wet weather. Frozen feet were particularly troublesome. Patton protested heatedly about COM Z's failure to provide enough blankets, overcoats, raincoats and waterproof overshoes. If thermal boots had arrived at front lines in early October, thousands of American soldiers would have avoided foot ailments which

13. Air Support for the Third Army's Autumn Operations

Third Army truck in flooded Moselle region (courtesy of NARA).

removed them from combat at a time when a severe shortage of riflemen developed.[16]

Bitter recriminations about army support services circulated among Allied commanders. Spaatz inspected the IX Air Service Command and noted that its commander "was not carrying out job as should be done."[17] As mentioned earlier in this narrative, Spaatz himself and Arnold were at fault for not establishing greater coordination among units that employed transport aircraft.

A large lake behind the German line posed a potential threat to future Third Army operations. Rains were filling it to high levels. Its water was contained by a dam near Dieuze. If the dam were blown during a Third Army offensive, released water could delay or isolate some of the attacking units. Air and ground planners made an unusual recommendation: XIX TAC should breach the dam with bombs prior to the Third Army's offensive. The 362 Fighter Group was chosen for the mission. On October 20, P-47s dived from 7000 feet into a storm of flak and dropped 1000-

pound bombs at 100 feet. Six hits broke open the dam and water rushed through the gap, flooding the surrounding lowlands. Some German units were trapped and later surrendered.[18]

During the relatively quiet period in October, the Third Army's rear area hummed with activity as COM Z brought supplies and equipment to support the next offensive. Trucks roared along roads reserved for military vehicles, carrying boats stacked like saucers, tanks, ammunition, clothing, rations and gasoline. Ordnance companies set up roadside stations to service vehicles. They patched tires to prolong their lives, and welded cleats to tracks of tanks to give them more traction.

The Allied supply crisis was not over. The amount of supplies unloaded at ports did not meet SHAEF's planning estimates: [19]

	August	*September*	*October*	*November*
Beaches	17,300	13,100	6,300	900
Cherbourg	8,500	10,400	11,800	14,000
Normandy & Brittany ports	4,300	5,800	4,400	3,700
Le Havre			2,000	4,800
Rouen			900	4,100
Totals	30,100	29,300	25,400	27,500
SHAEF's planning estimates	30,700	37,600	38,600	51,200
Deficits	600	8,300	13,200	23,700

Table 6. **Tons of Cargo Unloaded Daily**

Replacements arrived to fill the Third Army's ranks. Troops trained to learn how to cope with the difficult tasks that faced them when they penetrated the German frontier region. Special attention was given to ways to keep feet warm and dry.

14

The November Offensive

During the October pause in operations, the Third Army's staff made plans to launch an offensive as soon as supplies became adequate and SHAEF authorized it. The Third Army's morale improved in October with rest, replenishment of supplies and equipment, and arrival of replacement troops.

Patton visited troops and told them: "It is 132 miles to the Rhine from here, and if the army will attack with venom and desperate energy, it is more than probable that the war will end before we get to the Rhine. Therefore, when we attack, go like hell!"[1]

Patton decided to send XII Corps south of Metz toward the Rhine. It would drive from the Pont-â-Mousson area and bypass the strongest forts in the region. XX Corps would cross the Moselle at Thionville, take Metz and advance toward Mainz, on the Rhine 140 miles away. XV Corps was now a part of the Seventh Army.

Heavy rains of November were "Hitler's weather." Rain totals far exceeded averages for Lorraine. Miserable weather handicapped Allied air and ground operations, and added to troop discomfort.

The Ninth Air Force prepared to execute a formidable air campaign in support of the Third Army in November. From November 1 to 7, fighter-bombers flew 1000 sorties, attacking supply dumps, airfields, bridges and railroad yards. Medium bombers attacked forts and railroad bridges. When the offensive started on November 8, fighter-bombers attacked command posts, artillery batteries, troop concentrations and the usual interdiction targets on roads and railroads near the front.

On November 9 the Eighth Air Force dispatched a force of 1,120 heavy bombers to attack Metz forts and a marshalling yard at Saarbrücken. Although the Third Army would bypass most forts, it was still necessary to pummel their artillery positions. Radio beacons and a line of artillery shell bursts helped bombers identify front lines and avoid short bombings. Medium bombers attacked road junctions, barracks and an ordnance arsenal. Air reconnaissance provided information and photographs relative to important targets.[2]

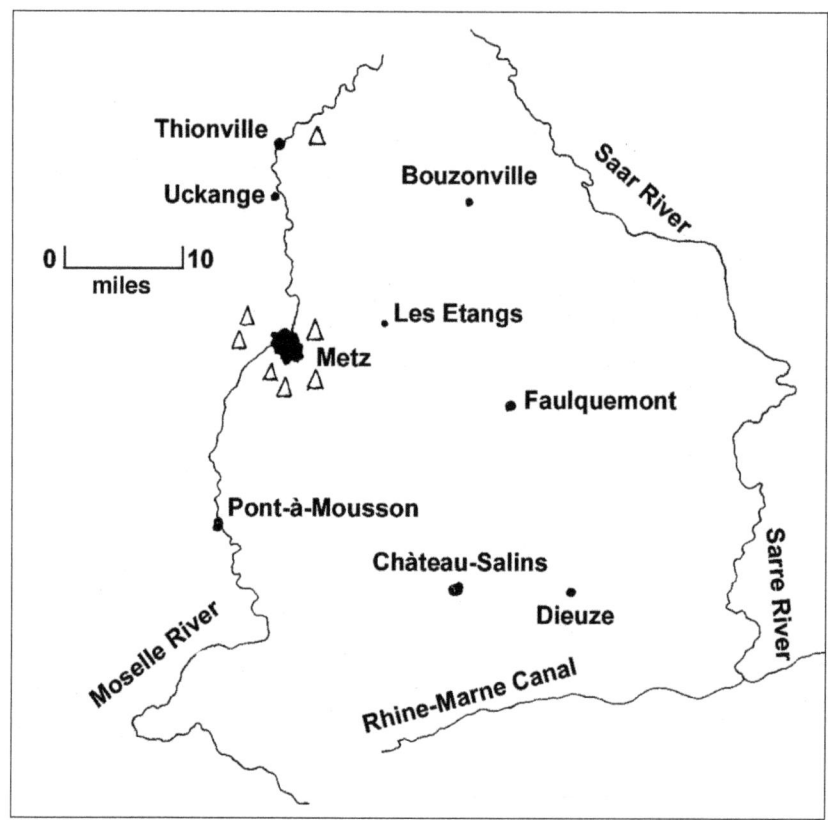

Map 9. Objectives of the Third Army in its November 1944 Offensive

COM Z made Herculean efforts to build up supply dumps to support the Third Army's November offensive. Truck convoys brought 35,600 troops and 179,000 tons of supplies. Fourteen tank-truck companies delivered 10 percent more gasoline than was requested. Signal companies laid 142 miles of field wire, 220 miles of spiral-four cable, and 966 miles of open wire on 45 miles of poles.[3]

Hitler had consistently supported his antiaircraft services. He believed they were essential to defend Germany against bombers, and could also be used in ground warfare. Now, as front lines moved closer to Germany, antiaircraft forces had a smaller area to defend. They became a greater menace to Allied air and ground forces. XIX TAC's pilots often reported that they had encountered flak that was "dense and accurate."

The German First Army occupied the area east of the Third Army's front lines. Its units were organized to conduct an elastic defense. The

14. The November Offensive

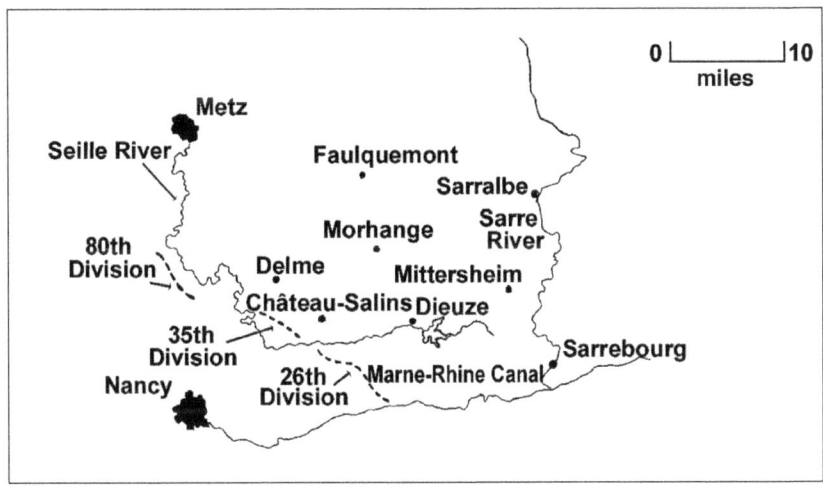

Map 10. XII Corps' Front, 8 November 1944

front line would be held by weak forces backed up by stronger units two or three kilometers behind them. Defensive positions had been strengthened by anti-tank ditches, trenches, pillboxes and minefields. Von Rundstedt sent reinforcements, which increased German strength to eight divisions and 285 tanks. Every village became a strong point. Road blocks and blown bridges delayed the Third Army. German intelligence units secured accurate information about the Third Army, most of it based on careless telephone and radio communications by American troops.[4]

The German Air Force was badly overmatched in numbers and quality. It concentrated on night operations and a few daylight attacks when the odds were in its favor. These tactics gave GAF pilots a better chance to survive, but they were often little more than a nuisance to the Allies. German air reconnaissance was abysmal.

Rain delayed the start of the November offensive. Patton waited three days for weather clear enough to permit the Ninth Air Force to operate, but he finally ordered the offensive to begin in a heavy downpour.

General Eddy ordered XII Corps' soldiers to leave their overshoes behind when they attacked. Many soldiers developed foot maladies when bitter cold followed a week of rain.

XII Corps planned to attack with the 35th, 80th and 26th Infantry Divisions, and the 4th and 6th Armored Divisions. All five divisions had had extensive experience in combat operations.

After infantry broke open the front, armor would drive through the gaps and create confusion in the enemy's rear areas. This kind of armor/

infantry operation required boldness and speed, but the ground was saturated, with mud so thick that tanks had to stay on hard-surfaced roads. German artillery had arranged to fire accurately on roads. Many roads were mined. Scarcity of usable bridges also slowed troop movements.

At 0600 on November 8, elements of three infantry divisions began to advance, with the 26th Division on the right, the 35th Division in the center, and the 80th Division on the left. Artillery fired more than 23,000 shells in support. Some artillery shells buried themselves in mud without exploding. XII Corps soon met stiff German resistance from heavy, accurate artillery fire, minefields, tank traps, pillboxes, and counterattacks. XIX TAC's fighter-bombers flew 471 sorties to soften defenses, but weather forced cancellation of most medium bomber missions.

Swollen rivers, flooded lowlands, mud and cold contributed substantially to XII Corps' difficulties. Soldiers modified tank tracks to improve traction.

Despite inclement weather and difficult terrain, the 26th Division achieved tactical surprise. It captured several bridges over the Seille and a small village that yielded 542 prisoners. In a three-day battle for a dominant hill, the 26th Division lost 478 men killed and wounded.[5]

The 35th Infantry Division crossed a tributary of the Seille on bridges captured before they could be blown, and others constructed by engineers. Before dark on November 9, the 35th Division captured two villages and more than 200 defenders.

When it attempted to clear the Forêt de Château-Salins, the 35th Division met fierce resistance. Not until November 11 did fighting slacken. When German troops began to withdraw they were hit hard by fighter-bombers of XIX TAC.

The 4th Armored Division moved through the bridgehead won by the 35th Infantry Division. Morhange was its initial objective. A task force of the 4th Armored rolled into a village four miles north of Dieuze on November 14, but was forced to withdraw after taking high losses from artillery fire.

The CCB of the 4th Armored Division moved north of the Forêt de Château-Salins on November 9. After some initial successes, it encountered a strong German position and became involved in a major tank battle. The CCB lost 15 tanks, 10 half-tracks, and three assault guns. The German force withdrew on November 12.[6]

On November 8 leading units of the 80th Infantry Division crossed the Seille River in assault boats. Before dark it secured ten bridges over the Seille and a bridgehead on the east shore. Heavy fighting took place on a ridge near Delme. XIX TAC's fighter-bombers attacked German positions on the ridge.[7]

The 6th Armored Division moved over ground gained by the 80th Infantry Division, using the only hard-surfaced road in the sector. As German troops began to retreat before these two divisions, Eddy urged their commanders to pursue the enemy to the limit of their divisions' endurance.

Weather, terrain obstacles, mined roads, blown bridges, and German opposition slowed the Third Army's progress, especially its armor. Snow blanketed the region during the night of November 12–13. Patton's troops had not received winter camouflage clothing. They made clear targets silhouetted against the new snow.

On the night of November 12–13, Eddy ordered the 26th and 35th Infantry Divisions to seize crossings over the Sarre River. The Sarre was the last major natural obstacle west of the Siegfried Line, which the Germans called the West Wall. It extended from the Netherlands to Switzerland along Germany's western frontier. It included 3000 concrete pillboxes and bunkers with cleared fields of fire, minefields, tank ditches, and trenches. After an attack by the 26th Division on November 18 penetrated the German line, the 4th Armored advanced toward Mittersheim. On November 20 the 26th Infantry and 4th Armored Divisions captured Dieuze. A few days later the 4th Armored occupied positions overlooking the Sarre. Casualties of the 26th Division in November were high—661 killed, 2,154 wounded and 2,898 ill.

In November the 35th Infantry and 6th Armored Divisions fought fierce, costly battles as they pushed eastward twenty-seven miles. The 35th Division captured 2309 prisoners. Its casualties totaled 349 killed, 1549 wounded and 115 missing. The 6th Armored lost 94 tanks, with 162 soldiers killed, 725 wounded and 47 missing.[8]

As November ended, XII Corps prepared to attack key positions on the Siegfried Line. Patton and Vandenberg hoped that air attacks would at least soften some of the many fortified positions in the region. Air attacks might only dent massive stone and concrete fortifications, but they would disrupt communications, depress morale of the German defenders, and encourage American troops.

XX Corps' field order of November 3 called for the destruction or capture of the Metz garrison without investiture or siege of the forts around the city. Bitter lessons from assaults on forts had taught the Third Army to avoid such operations if possible.

For the November offensive, XX Corps had the 5th, 90th and 95th Infantry Divisions, the 10th Armored Division, 21 battalions of artillery, three tank battalions, four antiaircraft artillery battalions, two squadrons of cavalry and eight engineer battalions.[9]

The 90th Division had fought in the hedgerows of Normandy, the Falaise pocket, Thionville, and Maizieres-les-Metz. It began its part in the November offensive with crossings of the Moselle. After weeks of rain, the river swirled in turbulent currents, overflowed its banks, and flooded the adjacent low areas. Engineers struggled to place floats called pontons in the choppy water. Flat-bottomed assault boats carried troops and supplies across the river. In the early morning hours of November 11, engineers completed a ponton bridge.

The 90th Division's attack surprised the enemy. The town of Koenigsmacker was quickly captured. The next day, artillery, mortar and automatic weapons fire hit the leading elements. The river channel was now 1.5 miles wide. Tanks could not cross it. Meager supplies came to the east shore in boats. Despite the difficult conditions, the 90th Division advanced. Troops fought without bridges, supplies, tanks, rest, dry clothing, or adequate rations. Fort Koenigsmacker fell after holding out for three days. During the next week the 90th Division repelled several counterattacks as it moved toward Metz. After eleven days of battle, the 90th Division met elements of the 5th Infantry Division and completed its part of the encirclement of Metz. The 90th Division lost 2300 officers and men in operations near the Moselle. Patton commended the division for executing "one of the epic river crossings of history."[10]

Soon after dark on November 8, engineers attached to the 95th Infantry Division crossed the Moselle near Uckange to clear minefields. Infantry followed and established a small bridgehead east of the river. Early the next morning more troops crossed the river in assault boats. Cold, rushing water and enemy artillery made river crossings in boats hazardous.

Liaison aircraft dropped medical supplies, sleeping bags, socks, food, gloves and ammunition into the besieged bridgehead. Two days after the attack began, the situation of the few troops on the east shore was precarious. No armored vehicles could cross the Moselle to expand the bridgehead. Troops were cold, wet and tired. Snow flurries added to their discomfort. In these conditions, many soldiers became sick. Engineers labored to construct bridges in frigid water under shelling.[11]

Reinforced by a battalion on November 13, 95th Division troops in the small bridgehead repelled repeated counter-attacks until a relief force of the 90th Division arrived. In hard fighting, the 95th Division cleared Thionville, finally secured a bridge over the Moselle, and expanded the bridgehead. A task force of the 95th Division helped clear Metz on November 16. With help from self-propelled 155 mm howitzers firing point-blank at the doors of a fort on the periphery of Metz, the 95th Division seized the fort and entered the city.¹²

While the 90th and 95th Divisions advanced north of Metz, the 5th Infantry Division launched a drive east of the Seille River on November 9 and made good progress. On November 13 Walker ordered the 5th Division to attack the garrison remaining in Metz.

German troops and officials began to withdraw from Metz, despite Hitler's orders to hold their positions to the last man. By November 17 the Third Army controlled the city. All resistance ended a few days later. Garrisons in the forts around Metz surrendered in the next few weeks as it became clear to them that there was little point in holding out.

For five days after the Third Army's offensive opened, the 10th Armored Division waited to cross the Moselle. Finally, working under mortar and artillery fire, the 1306th Engineer General Service Regiment constructed a Bailey bridge over the river near Thionville. It was the longest such bridge constructed in the ETO up to that time. The 10th Armored moved east of Metz to capture crossings over the Sarre River.¹³

After Metz was cleared of Germans, XX Corps advanced eastward toward the Sarre River. The terrain east of Metz contained no difficult barriers except high ground along the west bank of the Sarre. By nightfall on November 25, XX Corps' units were four miles from the river. Three days later the 90th and 95th Divisions moved into position to cross the river and establish bridgeheads.

In the late afternoon of December 2, a pilot of an artillery observation airplane spotted a bridge still intact in Saarlautern. The next day troops of the 95th Division crossed the river in assault boats shrouded by fog and surprised bridge guards. Engineer troops raced onto the bridge and cut demolition wires. German counterattacks failed to retake the bridge, and artillery fire did not knock it out. The 95th Division secured a bridgehead for a drive into the heart of the city.¹⁴

By December 15, despite atrocious weather, strong defenses and determined German resistance, the Third Army had seized almost the entire Saar region. It continued to operate virtually free of air attacks. The Eighth and Ninth Air Forces retained the air supremacy they had won in the first half of 1944.

Support services made crucial contributions to the Third Army in November. Engineers constructed over 4.5 miles of bridging, including 120 Bailey bridges, 111 treadway bridges, 64 timber spans and two heavy ponton bridges.

Signal companies laid 142 miles of field wire, 226 miles of cable and over 45 miles of pole-supported lines.

Medical personnel treated 4,587 cases of trench foot. Most of the affected soldiers could not return to duty for many weeks.[15]

Ninth Air Force photographic reconnaissance units performed tasks of major importance to the Third Army's November operations. They provided photographs that helped XIX TAC, IX Bomber Command, and the Third Army's artillery identify command posts, antiaircraft and artillery batteries, railroad yards, bridges, and fortified positions.[16]

The Allied supply crisis eased when ships began unloading cargoes at Antwerp at the end of November.

As the Third Army prepared to drive into Germany in December, events in the center of the Allied front forced it to change plans. Eisenhower told Patton that elements of the Third Army would be needed to help repel a powerful German counteroffensive that had burst through the Ardennes. Under Hitler's personal direction, German forces attacked toward the Meuse River, an effort they planned to follow with a drive to capture Antwerp. Several Allied divisions were hit hard. Some American units were surrounded, and others retreated in disarray. The strength of the counteroffensive and its early victories shocked Allied leaders and peoples who had hoped that Germany was near defeat.

15

The Drive to Bastogne

During November and December 1944, with their short periods of daylight and thick cloud cover, Ninth Air Force reconnaissance pilots had fewer opportunities to monitor enemy activities. These conditions, along with a policy of strict radio silence, helped Hitler build up a powerful panzer force east of the Ardennes undetected by the Allies. Air reconnaissance did report heavy motor vehicle, barge and rail traffic in the Rhine region. ULTRA intelligence also warned of German actions that appeared to be preparations for a counteroffensive. For reasons never explained, SHAEF did not issue warnings that a German offensive would probably begin soon.[1]

SHAEF believed it unlikely that a German attack would strike through the forested Ardennes region. This assumption motivated Bradley to hold the front in the area with only four divisions, two of them in dire need of rehabilitation after hard combat, a third untested in combat, and the fourth short one of its regiments.

Hitler held high hopes for the counteroffensive. The plan called for two armies to hit the weakest section of the First Army's line in the Ardennes with overwhelming strength, break open the front, cross the Meuse and wheel northward to capture Antwerp.

On December 16, eleven infantry and eight panzer divisions attacked on a 60-mile front in Belgium, opening large gaps in the Allied line. The strength of the German onslaught surprised SHAEF and discouraged Allied peoples and military personnel. They had been led to believe that the Germans would soon surrender. The German assault forces took control of a large part of an area formerly held by the First Army. It became known as the "Bulge."[2]

Eisenhower made some changes to cope with the crisis. He appointed Field Marshal Montgomery to direct two American armies temporarily. This decision infuriated Bradley and Patton.[3] SHAEF put IX and XXIX TACs under the operational control of the British 2nd Tactical Air Force. The Ninth Air Force switched the 365th, 367th and 368th Fighter Groups

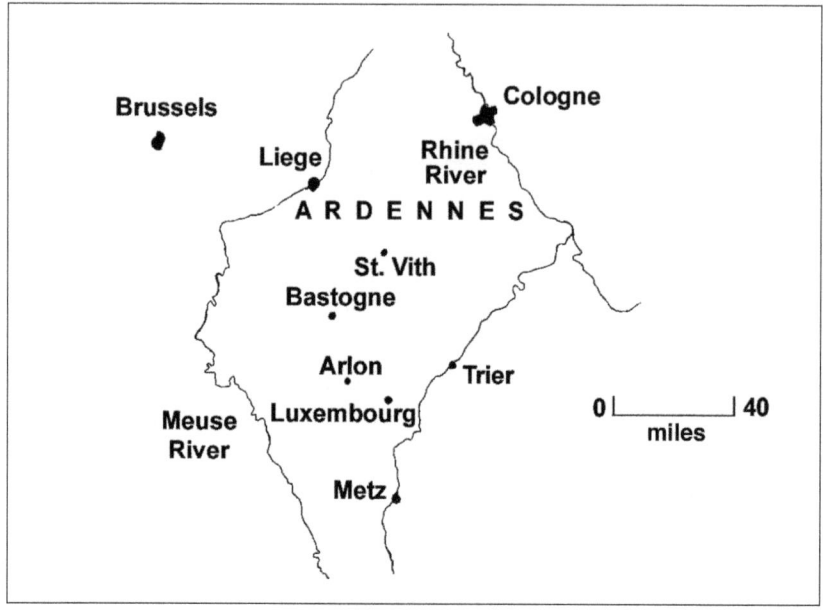

Map 11. Ardennes Area

to XIX TAC. The Eighth Air Force assigned a bombardment division and several P-51 groups to the Ninth Air Force.

Eisenhower ordered the 82nd and 101st Airborne Divisions to occupy key transportation centers in the path of the German drive. The 7th Armored Division moved forward to hold ground around St. Vith, a crucial road hub, where the 168th Engineer Combat Team and shattered infantry units fought hard. The defense of Bastogne by the 101st Airborne Division was one of the most dramatic of many heroic actions by American troops during the Battle of the Bulge.

Some American units in the VIII Corps area were surrounded, overrun or forced to retreat. Some surrendered. Stubborn resistance by American troops at key transportation centers slowed the German advance. U.S. Army engineer forces blew bridges and laid minefields to delay the enemy.[4]

Brigadier General Bruce Clarke, formerly commander of the CCA of the 4th Armored Division, now led a task force of the 7th Armored Division, and other troops he rallied, in hard fighting around St. Vith.

On December 19 Bradley ordered Patton to send part of the Third Army northward to strike at German forces in the Bulge, especially those that had the 101st Airborne Division surrounded in Bastogne. It was a dangerous and difficult maneuver, one that required planning and discipline

General Patton and staff in the Third Army's map room (courtesy of USAMHI).

of a high standard. Bradley, who was often critical of Patton, later described the Third Army's staff work as a "brilliant effort."

Patton rapidly organized a force under the control of III Corps, a unit new to the Third Army, to carry out the mission. III Corps consisted of the 26th and 80th Infantry, and 4th Armored Divisions. Patton gave the 4th Armored Division his close attention. He expected it to relieve Americans in Bastogne. He told the Fourth Armored's recently appointed commander, Major General Hugh Gaffey, to lead with tanks, followed by artillery, tank destroyers and armored engineers. The 4th Armored was short 21 medium tanks. No new ones were available to replace losses. Most of its operating tanks were in poor condition after months of hard use. One tank battalion lost 33 tanks from mechanical failures in the next few days. Tanks could move well on frozen fields but sometimes slid off icy roads into ditches.[5]

At 0430 on December 22, the CCB of the 4th Armored moved northward from an area east of Neufchâteau. By noon it was near Burnon, only seven miles from Bastogne. The CCA attacked on the right of the CCB and had to fight hard to overcome enemy resistance a few miles from Bastogne.[6]

Patton described the work of ordnance soldiers as outstanding. Soon after the Third Army received orders to wheel to the north, ordnance teams cleared roads to be used by ammunition trucks moving toward Bastogne. Ordnance teams winched hundreds of vehicles out of ditches.

On December 25 the CCR of the 4th Armored received orders to drive to Bastogne. Tanks and half-tracks of the 37th Tank Battalion, commanded by Lt. Col. Creighton W. Abrams, cleared Remonville, a village on the road from Neufchâteau to Bastogne. The next day the 37th Battalion moved toward Assenois, a town only a few miles from Bastogne. Thirteen batteries of artillery plastered Assenois to help the 37th Battalion clear it and move on.

At 1620 the 4th Armored Division made contact with the 101st Airborne Division in Bastogne. During the night of December 26–27, tanks of the 37th Tank Battalion escorted 40 trucks and 70 ambulances into Bastogne.[7] A biographer of Patton called the Third Army's Ardennes campaign the "sublime moment of his career." Patton described the drive to Bastogne as "the most brilliant operation we have thus far performed ... the outstanding achievement of this war."[8]

When German forces smashed through front lines on December 16, thick cloud cover concealed them from Allied air forces. During the next seven days, medium bombers of the Ninth Air Force operated only on December 18. Fighter-bombers of XIX TAC remained on the ground, except for a few sorties on December 19 and 21.

A few days before Christmas, a 5-day period of clear weather began. Leading German units were within five miles of the Meuse, but that was as close to the river as they would get. On December 23 the Ninth Air Force dispatched 624 medium bombers to attack bridges and road hubs in the Ardennes region. C-47s of IX Troop Carrier Command dropped 668,000 pounds of supplies to American troops in Bastogne. Von Rundstedt reported that attacks on bridges clogged traffic and stalled troop movements during the Ardennes counteroffensive.

XIX TAC flew 1,102 sorties in support of the Third Army on December 26–27. Three groups gave close ground support, two flew armed reconnaissance, and the 354th Fighter Group escorted C-47s on airlift missions to Bastogne. Fighter-bomber pilots had great difficulty identifying enemy road traffic because the Germans had captured many U.S. Army vehicles.[9]

Allied air forces hit the enemy with devastating power whenever weather was clear enough to fly. Operations of the 406th Fighter Group are representative of the performance of fighter-bombers during the Ardennes battles. In the early morning hours of December 23 it attacked German units near Bastogne. Throughout daylight hours it bombed and strafed enemy vehicles and positions. The 406th Group also used high-velocity aircraft rockets to advantage in these engagements. During five days the Group's P-47s destroyed or damaged 13 enemy aircraft, 610 motor vehicles, 194 armored vehicles, and many horse-drawn wagons, bridges, and supply dumps.[10]

As the new year began, German forces started an orderly retreat from the Ardennes salient. American air and ground forces had broken the German counteroffensive.

After the Ardennes battles, Montgomery spoke to journalists and gave himself and British forces a major share of the credit for the outcome. "I employed the whole power of the British Group of Armies," he declared.[11] He implied that American commanders had been unable to organize an effective defense until he took charge.

In fact, few British troops fought in the Battle of the Bulge. The British suffered some 500 casualties, the Americans 70,000. The German drive had been slowed, disrupted and defeated by American ground and air forces before Montgomery's orders had an appreciable impact on the battle. In fact, many American officers perceived Montgomery's recommendations to be timid and pusillanimous.

In reaction to Montgomery's bluster, Bradley told Eisenhower: "...After what has happened I cannot serve under Montgomery. If he is to be put in command of all ground forces, you must send me home, for if Montgomery goes in over me, I will have lost the confidence of my command."[12]

Eisenhower quickly placated Bradley and other Americans. He removed American armies from Montgomery's direction.

General Marshall sent Eisenhower a firm recommendation about Montgomery and his aspirations for higher command: "They may or may not have brought to your attention articles in certain London papers proposing a British deputy commander for all your ground forces.... My feeling is this: under no circumstances make any concessions of any kind whatsoever."[13]

Churchill became aware of American resentment about Montgomery's statements. He spoke about the controversy in Parliament: "I have seen it suggested that the terrific battle which has been proceeding since December 16 on the American front is an Anglo-American battle. In fact, however, the United States troops have done almost all the fighting, and have suffered almost all the losses...."

In a message to President Roosevelt, Churchill wrote: "I most cordially congratulate you on the extraordinary gallantry which your troops have shown in all this battle, particularly at Bastogne and two other places ... many troops of the First Army have fought to the end, holding crossroads in the area of incursion...."[14]

16

Evaluations of Air Support for the Third Army

Effective use of air power in close cooperation with ground forces was one of the most significant achievements of the Army Air Forces in World War II. To employ fighters, bombers and transports effectively on close support missions, the AAF had to have many support services, such as ordnance, engineering, communications, and aircraft maintenance.

XIX TAC compiled a summary of its experiences in the campaigns in Northwest Europe in 1944–45. The quality and amount of close air cooperation with ground forces varied with the rate of advance of the armies. When armored columns were moving rapidly, tactical air forces helped them eliminate obstacles. In a stable ground situation, fighter-bombers did not have to attack targets that artillery could handle. Air units had other obligations that could divert them from close air support, such as special tasks assigned by SHAEF, missions to maintain air superiority, and interdiction.

The morale of airmen working with ground forces often improved as they saw definite results of their efforts. Commanders of ground forces often reminded airmen that the presence of Allied aircraft over the front boosted the morale of their troops and depressed that of the enemy.

Ground forces invariably commended armored-column cover. Fighter-bomber pilots bombed and strafed targets accurately and rarely hit Allied troops. Effectiveness of armored-column cover improved as air and ground personnel gained experience with it, and better radio, radar and rocket equipment came into use.

In its interdiction campaigns, XIX TAC destroyed a wide range of targets, including motor vehicles, wagons, supply depots, railroad yards, tracks, trains, barges, bridges and command centers. The XIX TAC report complained that the "fruits of the program of interdiction and harassment would have been considerably larger had it not been interrupted by concentration of fighter-bomber effort at Brest, a strongly fortified port."[1]

Airmen and ground commanders often disagreed about target selection. Fortifications were not likely to be damaged much by air bombardment, but airmen were often ordered to attack them. Ground forces claimed that such attacks disrupted enemy communications, stunned enemy troops and forced them to seek shelter. German artillery often ceased firing when fighter-bombers were in the area. To achieve benefits from air bombardments, Allied soldiers had to attack soon after the last bomb fell. This required a high level of air-ground coordination.

Allied army commanders often requested carpet bombings to start offensives. Airmen protested that these actions were a wasteful misuse of air power. They had not been trained nor equipped to execute carpet bombings. During some carpet bombings, bombs fell on Allied troops. Heavy and medium bombers did not have sufficient bombing accuracy to preclude such accidents. To reduce the probability of mishaps during carpet bombings, friendly troops withdrew thousands of yards from target areas. This meant that they often had to fight to regain ground from which they had withdrawn.

The importance of air reconnaissance was recognized by both air and ground personnel. The XIX TAC report asserted that, "Direct and close control of a Reconnaissance Group, including both photo and visual reconnaissance as well as artillery adjustment [of fire], is absolutely essential to the proper operation of a Tactical Air Command cooperating with an Army."

Allied air forces had a few night fighters but they were not effective. This was one of the most serious weaknesses in AAF operations. If the AAF had acquired aircraft that could attack ground forces effectively at night, the Germans would have had much more difficulty moving supplies, equipment and personnel.

Effective air-ground coordination requires complex communications equipment and skilled personnel. Signal companies faced difficult supply and transportation problems during the Third Army's rapid drive across France. XIX TAC set up a small signal detachment composed of key personnel which moved forward with cable and radio equipment in close contact with Third Army headquarters. Both air and ground personnel violated rules for radio transmissions, thus endangering security and overloading channels.

XIX TAC's mobility was severely curtailed by lack of transportation and airfields near front lines. Ninth Air Force training anticipated the crucial need for mobility, but shortages of trucks, ports, railroads, bridges, roads and transport aircraft handicapped it. Early in the Battle of France it became necessary for the Allies to curtail interdiction programs—destruction of bridges, railroads, and other transportation installations. It was always difficult for the Ninth Air Force to estimate whether interdiction caused more problems for itself and the armies it supported than for the Germans.

IX Troop Carrier Command and the Eighth Air Force responded with skill and energy to SHAEF's orders to transport supplies to the armies. Employment of bomber and transport aircraft in "trucking" required modification of equipment and training of personnel.

The First Allied Airborne Army had its training interrupted in August because IX Troop Carrier Command was assigned to deliver supplies. Many AAF commanders believed it was unwise to take highly trained airmen and airborne troops out of combat operations for this purpose. The War Department criticized Eisenhower when airborne divisions waited on the sidelines for airplanes, or were used for long periods as infantry.

Air supply of American ground forces suffered from a lack of central direction. The AAF failed to anticipate demands for air supply to the extent that became necessary. Despite this failure, IX Troop Carrier Command and the Eighth Air Force delivered crucial supplies to the Third Army in the September-November period. Patton's divisions were six hundred miles from Normandy beaches and ports. Transportation networks in France were in bad condition at this time.[2]

A report by an AAF Operational Research Section summarized some of the lessons learned by tactical air commands in the European Theater of Operations. Fighter-bombers could carry bombs of weights ranging from 100 to 1000 pounds. The type of bomb employed—fragmentation, incendiary, armor-piercing, high explosive, napalm—varied according to the objectives of a mission. A few squadrons could fire high-velocity rockets.[3]

The success of a mission often depended on selection of appropriate bomb fuses. It was one of the lessons that fighter-bomber groups had difficulty learning. Fuses determined the location of the bomb's explosive force and thus its effectiveness.

To bomb effectively, air staffs had to understand the characteristics of targets. Fighter-bombers sometimes dropped bombs too small to destroy their targets. The AAF executed an intensive track-cutting campaign but much of the effort was wasted. Pilot claims about track-cutting were unreliable. Bombs did little damage to rails, and many bombs missed their targets completely. Repair of railroad tracks required crater-filling and repositioning of rails. To maximize the size of craters, ORS analysts recommended that fighter-bombers use the largest bombs they could carry.

Destruction of abutments caused the most difficult bridge-repair problems, but they were difficult to damage with bombs. Bridge piers were hard to hit. To bomb a bridge effectively, airmen had to use bombs with fuses that caused explosive forces to impact the most vulnerable and critical points. The Ninth Air Force often failed to do this.

Interdiction complicated German efforts to supply and move armies both in battle and in retreat. Destruction of French roads and railroads caused the Germans to abandon many stockpiles. However, an ORS report claimed that the Ninth Air Force had not achieved the general objective of its interdiction efforts: "The results of these attacks have been more of a harassing nature, for isolation [of a battle area] was probably never attained even once."[4] Clearly, interdiction needed much more study and better execution than it received in OVERLORD.

After the surrender of Germany, General Spaatz asked General Bradley to respond to a questionnaire about air-ground cooperation in Overlord. Bradley replied: "In this campaign, the recurring process of massing our divisions, forcing a breakthrough and the subsequent exploitation of our mobility to encircle and defeat the enemy demanded almost complete air superiority to overcome our sensitiveness in supply, reserves, and the necessity for full use of road and rail communications."[5]

Bradley believed that interdiction of a battle area was important, but airmen too often gave it priority over close support of ground forces. This, according to Bradley, was only one example of the AAF's "slavish" adherence to impractical air doctrine.

Bradley cited air activities that were especially valuable to ground forces:

- armored column cover
- reconnaissance
- air-ground liaison

It was a curious omission that he did not mention air supply.

"I cannot overemphasize the importance of a careful selection of tactical air party officers for our Corps and divisions," Bradley wrote. "In the few cases where this personnel have not been wholly capable, there has temporarily resulted either serious misunderstanding by our ground commanders of the air force role or the submission of air requests which were neither tactically sound nor beneficial to our troops."

Bradley criticized medium bomber operations. IX Bomber Command required too much time to respond to requests for close support, and rejected some that were crucial to ground forces. Medium bombers would have been more useful, he believed, if they had been directed by the tactical air commands. This recommendation ignored the facts that medium bombers had missions other than to support ground forces, and that air forces should have central direction.

Although carpet bombings had caused casualties to his troops, Bradley believed that it was a valuable offensive tactic: "I realize that the effect of this type of bombing has been a controversial matter, but while the casualty rate on [German] personnel may not be high there is no doubt as to the paralysis to personnel and communications caused by this tremendous shock effect."

Soon after Germany's surrender, Bradley established an "Air Effects" committee to collect the opinions of his army, corps, and division commanders about air support their units had received. They were unanimous in their approval of fighter-bombers. These aircraft "...ranged forward on rail and road-cutting missions, harassed troop concentrations, strafed and bombed enemy columns on foot or in motor vehicles or rail cars, harried and delayed enemy movements of troops, equipment and supplies." The ground-forces commanders appreciated air reconnaissance. It helped them strike hard at weak points, strengthen offensives, and anticipate enemy moves.[6]

Bradley and many of his fellow officers paid lip service to AAF strategic bombing. They understood that bombing Germany's vital industries cut sharply into its ability to wage war, but they believed the costs were too high. Although they appreciated the benefits of air supremacy, they did not agree that it was necessary to wage an expensive strategic bombing campaign to achieve it. They claimed that the tactical air forces could maintain air superiority over a battle area. Next to this comment, in the margin of his copy of the report, the commander of the Eighth Bomber Command wrote: "Dangerous conclusion."

The GAF was decimated by the battles it fought to blunt strategic bombing. Allied heavy bombers blasted oil refineries and thereby caused fuel shortages in all segments of the German war machine. A shortage of aviation gasoline forced the GAF to cut flight training. Pilots graduated who were in general less competent than the AAF and RAF pilots they met in combat. The outcome for the GAF was impotence.

The committee expanded on Bradley's criticism of interdiction: "Closer coordination and better logistical planning of interdiction programs would have in most cases, saved a certain amount of useless destruction of transportation facilities which would have later been helpful to our own forces."

One of the reasons for excellent air-ground coordination between the Third Army and the XIX Tactical Air Command was the friendship of

Patton and Weyland. Patton also maintained good relations with other air commanders. Spaatz, Doolittle and Vandenberg served with Patton in the North African and Sicilian campaigns. They admired him and knew that he appreciated air power. They tended to react positively to his requests for air support.

Patton often praised the Army Air Forces. In a letter to Marshall, he wrote: "The cooperation between the Third Army and the XIX Tactical Air Command ... has been the finest example of the ground and air working together that I have ever seen...."[7]

To Arnold, Patton wrote: "For about 250 miles I have seen the calling cards of the fighter-bombers, which are bullet markets in the pavement and burned tanks and trucks in the ditches...."[8]

In General Orders of the Third Army, January 1, 1945, Patton sent a message: "To the officers and men of the Third Army and to our comrades of the XIX Tactical Air Command:

> From the bloody corridor at Avranches, to Brest, thence across France to the Saar, over the Saar into Germany, and now on to Bastogne, your record has been one of continuous victory. Not only have you invariably defeated a cunning and ruthless enemy, but also you have overcome by your indomitable fortitude every aspect of terrain and weather."[9]

After the war, Weyland stated to an interviewer: "General George S. Patton was the finest field commander I have ever known.... Largely because of his prevailing leadership, relations between Third Army and XIX TAC were characterized by complete confidence in the other's abilities...."[10]

A military history of World War II sums up the results of the Battle of France:

> In seven weeks [after August 1] the Western Allies liberated much of western Europe and had destroyed or put to rout five German armies. The campaign vindicated the Overlord plan, our Army's tactical doctrine, and the doctrine of the Army Air Forces.... the faster you move and the harder you hit the fewer your casualties will be — a theory vigorously propounded and applied by General Patton."[11]

Glossary

AAF: Army Air Forces
AEAF: Allied Expeditionary Air Forces
AFSC: Air Force Service Command
CCA: Combat Command A
CCS: Combined Chiefs of Staff committee
Cobra: codename for the First U.S. Army offensive, July 1944
Enigma: German machine to encipher and decipher coded messages
ETO: European Theater of Operations
Fortitude: codename for an Allied deception operation
GAF: German Air Force
Mission: an operation to accomplish a specific objective
Market-Garden: codename for the Allied operation to seize a bridgehead over the Rhine River near Arnhem
ORS: Operational Research Section
Panzer: German armored force
PHS: Prefabricated Hessian Surfacing runway surface material
PSP: Pierced Steel Plank runway surface material
RAF: Royal Air Force
Resistance: irregular French military forces
SHAEF: Supreme Headquarters Allied Expeditionary Forces
SMT: Square Mesh Track runway surface material
Sortie: single operation of a single aircraft
TAC: Tactical Air Command
TCC: Troop Carrier Command
TUSA: Third United States Army
Ultra: codename for Allied program to intercept and decrypt German messages enciphered by Enigma machines
USSTAF: United States Strategic Air Forces

Notes

Archives frequently cited in the notes are identified by the following abbreviations:

LOC   Library of Congress Manuscript Division
NARA   U.S. National Archives
USAFHRA   U. S. Air Force Historical Research Agency
USAMHI   U.S. Army Military History Institute

Titles of works and names of people are shortened after their first appearance.

Introduction

1. Dwight D. Eisenhower to Winston S. Churchill, April 5, 1944, Alfred D. Chandler, ed., *The War Years*, vol. 3 of *The Papers of Dwight David Eisenhower* (Baltimore, Md.: The Johns Hopkins University Press, 1970), p. 1809.

2. Eisenhower, *Crusade in Europe* (Garden City, N.Y.: Doubleday, 1948), p. 56.

3. Carl A. Spaatz, diary, February 19, 1944, box 14, Spaatz Papers, LOC.

4. E. J. Kingston-McCoughry, *The Direction of War* (New York: Praeger, 1955), p. 121.

5. Charles Messinger, *Bomber Harris* (New York: St. Martin's Press, 1984), p. 157.

6. Carlos D'Este, *Patton: A Genius for War* (New York: Harper Collins, Publishers, 1995).

7. Henry H. Arnold to Director of Air Support, December 28, 1942, box 38, Arnold Papers, LOC.

8. Arnold to Spaatz, April 14, 1944, box 14, Spaatz Papers, LOC.

9. Arnold to Lewis Brereton, February 26, 1944, box 105, Arnold Papers, LOC.

10. Omar N. Bradley, *A Soldier's Story* (New York: Henry Holt and Company, 1951), p. 250.

11. Lewis Brereton, *The Brereton Diaries* (New York: William Morrow, 1946), pp. 265–268.

Chapter 1

1. Bradley, *Soldier's Story*, appendix.
2. *Ibid.*, p. 445.
3. Martin Blumenson, *The U.S. Army in World War II: Breakout and Pursuit* (Washington, D.C.: Center of Military History, 1961), p.356.
4. William Donahue, T. Cunningham, H. Pattison, *Clarke of St. Vith* (Cleveland, Ohio: Dillon, Liederbach, 1974) p. 24.
5. Blumenson, *Breakout and Pursuit*, p. 363.
6. *Ibid.*, p. 365.
7. Eisenhower, *Crusade in Europe*, p. 192.
8. Harry C. Butcher, *My Three Years with Eisenhower* (New York: Simon & Schuster, 1946), p. 667.
9. Blumenson, *Breakout and Pursuit*, p. 370.
10. *Ibid.*, pp. 374–375.
11. *Ibid.*, p. 384.
12. 6th Armored Division After-Action report, RG–407 NARA.
13. Combat record of the 6th Armored Division, 585.06A, USAFHRA.
14. AAF Evaluation Board report, *Effectiveness of Third Phase Tactical Air Operations in the European Theater of Operations*, August 1945, 138.4–36, USAFHRA, p. 309.
15. Ninth Air Force report, "Major Changes of Tactics and Techniques Within the Ninth Air Force," January 22, 1945, 533.549–1, USAFHRA.
16. AAF Evaluation board report, "Effectiveness...," p. 311.
17. Robert Aron, *France Reborn* (New York: Charles Scribner's Sons, 1964), p. 130.
18. William B. Dreux, *No Bridges Blown* (Notre Dame, Ind.: University of Notre Dame Press, 1971), p. 229.
19. Aron, *France Reborn*, p. 133.
20. *Ibid.*

Chapter 2

1. U.S. Army, *Field Manual 100–20*. July 1943.
2. O. P. Weyland oral history transcript, K239.0512–813, USAFHRA, p. 58.
3. Ninth Air Force report, "Three Types of Interdiction Targets," July 22, 1944, 533.454–3, USAFHRA.
4. RAF report, "Interrogation of Oberst Hoeffner by a Senior RAF Officer," box 134, Spaatz Papers, LOC.
5. Quesada to W. W. Momeyer, August 22, 1944, box 1, Quesada Papers, LOC.
6. *Ibid.*
7. Brereton, *Diaries*, p. 281.
8. "AEAF Historical Record and Diary," AIR 37/1436, PRO.

Chapter 3

1. AAF Evaluation Board report to AAF headquarters, September 25, 1944, box 164, Spaatz Papers, LOC.
2. *Ibid.*
3. Weyland oral history, p. 14.
4. *Ibid.*
5. Quesada oral history transcript, pp. 11–15, USAMHI.
6. AAF Evaluation Board report, "Tactics and Techniques Developed by the U.S. Tactical Air Commands in the ETO," March 1, 1945, 138.4-33, USAFHRA.
7. William R. Dunn, *Fighter Pilot* (Lexington: University of Kentucky Press, 1982), p. 120.
8. AAF Evaluation Board report, "Tactics and Techniques...," pp. 4–5
9. AAF Evaluation Board report, "Effectiveness of Third Phase...," p. 307.
10. *Ibid.*, p. 308.
11. *Ibid.*
12. AAF Evaluation Board report, "Tactics and Techniques...," p. 5.

Chapter 4

1. Hans Speidel, *Invasion 1944* (Chicago: Henry Regnery Company, 1950), p. 130.
2. Wladyslaw Kozaczuk, *Enigma* (Frederick, Md.: University Publications of America, Inc., 1984).
3. M. C. Helfers, diary, Helfers Papers, Archives and Museum, Citadel, Charleston, S.C.
4. Ralph Bennett, *Ultra in the West* (New York: Charles Scribner's Sons, 1979), p. 115.
5. Leigh-Mallory to Eisenhower, November 1944, box 104, Spaatz Papers, LOC.
6. Leigh-Mallory, *Despatch*, box 104, Spaatz Papers, LOC.
7. Blumenson, *Breakout and Pursuit*, p. 492.
8. W. F. Craven and J. L. Cate, eds. *Europe: ARGUMENT to V-E Day, January 1944 to May 1945*, vol. 3 of *The Army Air Forces in World War II* (Chicago: University of Chicago Press, 1951), p. 249.
9. George S. Patton, Jr., *War as I Knew It* (Boston: Houghton-Mifflin Company, 1947), p. 99.
10. Blumenson, *Breakout and Pursuit*, p. 567.
11. *Ibid.*, p. 559.
12. Operations report, XX Corps, 220-0-30, RG 407, NARA.
13. Weyland oral history transcript, p. 78.
14. Historical records of the 362 Fighter Group, GP-362-FI-HI, USAFHRA.
15. George S. Patton, Jr., *The Patton Papers*, Martin Blumenson, ed. (Boston: Houghton-Mifflin Company, 1974), p. 517.
16. Ninth Air Force report, "Organization of Reconnaissance Aviation in the Ninth Air Force," 533.626A, USAFHRA.

17. Historical records of the Tenth Photographic Reconnaissance Group, GP-10-RCN-HI, USAFHRA.
18. *Ibid.*
19. Craven, W. F., and J. L. Cate, eds. *Men and Planes*, vol. 6 of *The Army Air Forces in World War II* (Chicago: University of Chicago Press, 1951), p. 197.
20. Ninth Air Force headquarters report, August 14, 1944, 537.332, USAFHRA.
21. Tom Ivie, *Aerial Reconnaissance* (Fallbrook, Calif.: Aero Publishers, 1981), p. 65.

Chapter 5

1. Robert M. Lee, "History of IX Engineer Command," Lee Collection, 168.609–41, USAFHRA.
2. Gail Wright, *Battalion History*, published by the 832 Aviation Engineers Battalion, 1945, pp. 33–35.
3. AAF Evaluation Board report, "Effectiveness of Third Phase...," p. 119.
4. Lloyd F. Latendresse, *History of IX Engineer Command* (Weisbaden, Germany: privately printed, 1945), pp. 88–89.
5. Craven and Cate, *Europe: Argument to V-E Day*, p. 569.
6. Latendresse, *History of IX Engineer Command*, p. 87.
7. Historical records of the 14th Liaison Squadron, SQ-LIA-14-HI, USAFHRA.
8. Alfred M. Beck, Abe Bortz, Charles W. Lynch, Lida Mays, Ralph F. Weld, *Corps of Engineers: the War Against Germany* (Washington, D.C.: Center of Military History, 1985), p. 400.
9. Ninth Air Force report, "Effectiveness of Tactical Air Operations," August 14, 1944, 533.332, USAFHRA.
10. XIX TAC report, "Tactical Air Operations in Europe," 537.04A, USAFHRA.
11. Ninth Air Force directive, August 14, 1944, 533.454–3, USAFHRA.
12. G. R. Thompson and Dixie R. Harris, *The Signal Corps* (Washington, D.C.: Center of Military History, 1966), pp. 119–120.
13. Blumenson, *Breakout and Pursuit*, p. 349.
14. Elton F. Hammond, "Signals for Patton," *Signals*, September-October 1947, p. 10.
15. Thompson and Harris, *Signal Corps*. p. 120.
16. Ninth Air Force memorandum, November 7, 1944, 533.4501, USAFHRA.
17. XIX TAC report, "Tactical Air Operations in Europe."

Chapter 6

1. Blumenson, *Breakout and Pursuit*, p. 497.
2. XIX TAC intelligence summary, August 10, 1944, 537.306A, USAFHRA.
3. Henry Maule, *Out of the Sand* (London: Oldhams Books, Ltd., 1966), p. 197.

4. *Patton Papers*, p. 508.
5. C. P. Stacey, *Canadian Army, 1939–1945* (Ottawa: King's Printer, 1948), p. 198.
6. Bradley, *Soldier's Story*, p. 375.
7. Leigh-Mallory, *Despatch*, p. 60.
8. Bradley, *Soldier's Story*, p. 377.
9. Blumenson, *Breakout and Pursuit*, p. 509.
10. Bradley, *Soldier's Story*, p. 377.
11. Forrest C. Pogue, *Supreme Command* (Washington, D.C.: Center of Military History, 1996), p. 214.
12. Blumenson, *Breakout and Pursuit*, p. 529.
13. *Ibid.*, p. 527.
14. Milton Shulman, *Defeat in the West* (New York: Dutton, 1948), p. 158.
15. Blumenson, *Breakout and Pursuit*, p. 555.
16. AAF Evaluation Board report, "Effectiveness of Third Phase...," pp. 127–128.
17. Leigh-Mallory, *Despatch*, p. 59.
18. AAF Evaluation Board report, "Effectiveness of Third Phase...," p. 128.
19. James M. Gavin, *On to Berlin* (New York: Viking Press, 1978), p. 131.
20. Blumenson, *Battle of the Generals* (New York: Morrow, 1993), p. 210.
21. Patton, diary, August 15, 1944, *Patton Papers*, box 28, LOC.
22. Eisenhower, "Supreme Commander's Dispatch," January 1945, box 104, Spaatz Papers, LOC.

Chapter 7

1. Hobart R. Gay, diary, Gay Papers, USAMHI.
2. Historical records of the 362 Fighter Group, USAFHRA.
3. AAF report, *Ninth Air Force in the European Theater of Operations, April to November 1944*, 101–36, USAFHRA.
4. XIX TAC operations reports, August 1944, 537.450, USAFHRA.
5. Blumenson, *Breakout and Pursuit*, p. 572.
6. *Ibid.*, p. 575.
7. Pogue, *Supreme Command*, p. 217.
8. AAF Evaluation Board report, *Effectiveness of Third Phase Operations.*
9. Hans Von Luck, *Panzer Commander* (New York: Praeger, 1989), p. 166.
10. Blumenson, *Breakout and Pursuit*, p. 670.
11. AAF Evaluation Board report, "German Army Crosses the Seine," June 3, 1945, 138.4–39, USAFHRA.
12. Craven and Cate, *Europe: Argument...*, p. 281.
13. Blumenson, *Breakout and Pursuit*, p. 583.
14. AAF Evaluation Board report, "German Army Crosses the Seine."
15. Blumenson, *Breakout and Pursuit*, p. 598.
16. *Ibid.*, p. 603.
17. Bradley, *Soldier's Story*, p. 392.

18. Blumenson, *Breakout and Pursuit*, pp. 626–627.
19. XIX TAC operations report, August 1944, 537.450, USAFHRA.
20. Henry H. Arnold, *Global Mission* (New York: Harper, 1949), p. 520.

Chapter 8

1. Blumenson, *Breakout and Pursuit*, p. 563.
2. Corps Personnel, *XX Corps: Its History and Service in World War II* (Osaka, Japan: XX Corps Association, 194?), p. 83.
3. XX Corps operations report, "Normandy and France," RG 407, 220-0-30, NARA.
4. Donahue, Cunningham and Pattison, *Clarke of St. Vith*, p. 33.
5. Hanson Baldwin, *Tiger Jack* (Fort Collins, Colo.: Old Army Press, 1979), p. 21.
6. Donahue et al., *Clarke of St. Vith*, p. 45.
7. *Ibid.*
8. Baldwin, Tiger Jack, p. 69.

Chapter 9

1. Historical records of the 362 Fighter Group, USAFHRA.
2. Blumenson, *Breakout and Pursuit*, p. 646.
3. *Ibid.*, pp. 636–637.
4. Craven and Cate, *Europe: ARGUMENT*, p. 263.
5. Spaatz, diary, September 3, 1944, box 16, Spaatz Papers, LOC.
6. XIX TAC operations report, August 1944, 537.450, USAFHRA.
7. VIII Corps Report, "Battle of Brest," 585.106, USAFHRA.
8. AAF Evaluation Board report, *Effectiveness of Third Phase Operations*," p. 17.
9. Ninth Air Force ORS report 41, October 10, 1944, 533.3101, USAFHRA.
10. *Ibid.*
11. Craven and Cate, *Europe: ARGUMENT*, p. 263.
12. Frank J. Price, *Troy H. Middleton* (Baton Rouge: Louisiana State University Press, 1974), p. 201.
13. Blumenson, *Battle of the Generals*, p. 537.
14. Bradley, *Soldier's Story*, p. 367.
15. Patton, *Papers*, p. 532.
16. Craven and Cate, *Europe: ARGUMENT*, p. 555.
17. Pogue, *Supreme Command*, p. 260.
18. Martin Van Crevald, *Supplying War* (New York: Cambridge University Press, 1977), p. 216.
19. Hobart Gay, diary, August 29, 1944, Papers, USAMHI.
20. Van Crevald, *Supplying War*, p. 215.
21. Roland G. Ruppenthal, *U.S. Army in World War II: Logistical Support of*

the Armies, September 1944 — May 1945 (Washington, D.C.: Center of Military History, 1995), pp. 577–580.

22. Eisenhower to Bradley, September 28, 1944, *Papers*, p. 2199.

23. John Kennedy Ohl, *Supplying the Troops* (De Kalb: Northern Illinois University Press, 1994), p. 230.

24. Eisenhower, *Crusade in Europe*, p. 174.

25. Joseph Bykofsky and Harold Larson, *U.S. Army in World War II: The Transportation Corps: Operations Overseas* (Washington, D.C.: Office of the Chief of Military History, 1957), pp. 332–334.

26. Historical records of the Ninth Air Force Service Command, 560.461A and 540.02, USAFHRA.

27. USSTAF report: "Plan for Supplying by Air an Armored Force Advancing: Case I Across Northern France and the Low Countries; Case II Eastward from the Paris Area toward the Rhine," box 145, Spaatz Papers, LOC.

28. Historical records of IX AFSC, 560.461, USAFHRA.

Chapter 10

1. Craven and Cate, *Europe: ARGUMENT*, p. 277.
2. Arnold, *Global Mission*, pp. 520–521.
3. Bradley, *Soldier's Story*, p. 402.
4. Craven and Cate, *Europe: ARGUMENT*, p. 580
5. Martin Wolfe, *Green Light* (Washington, D.C.: Center for Air Force History, 1993), p. 233.
6. Craven and Cate, *Europe: ARGUMENT*, p. 561.
7. Historical records of the 467th Bombardment Group, USAFHRA.
8. Arthur Tedder, *With Prejudice* (Boston: Little, Brown, 1966), p. 598.
9. Doolittle to Spaatz, September 28, 1944, box 16, Spaatz Papers, LOC.
10. Craven and Cate, *Europe: ARGUMENT*, p. 562.
11. Austin J. Buchanan, *438th Troop Carrier Group in World War II* (Baldwin, Mich.: privately published, 1990), p. 34.
12. USSTAF report, "Plan for Supplying by Air an Armored Force."
13. Spaatz to Arnold, September 12, 1944, box 16, Spaatz Papers, LOC.

Chapter 11

1. Eisenhower to Marshall, August 24, 1944, *Papers*, pp. 2092–2093.
2. Eisenhower to commanders, September 4, 1944, box 18, Spaatz Papers, LOC.
3. Eisenhower to Montgomery, September 5, 1944, *Papers*, p. 2120.
4. *Ibid.*, p. 2119.
5. Roland G. Ruppenthal, "Logistics and the Broad-Front Strategy," *Command Decisions*, Kent Roberts, ed. (U.S. Army Center of Military History, 1960), pp. 419–428.

6. Eisenhower to commanders, September 13, 1944, *Papers*, pp. 2136–2137.
7. *Ibid.*, p. 2133.
8. Bradley, *Soldier's Story*, p. 416.
9. Craven and Cate, *Europe: ARGUMENT*, p. 604.
10. Martin Middlebrook, *Arnhem 1944* (San Francisco: Westview Press, 1994), p. 460.
11. Brereton, *Diaries*, p. 371.
12. James M. Gavin to Paul Williams, September 25, 1944, box 176, Spaatz Papers, LOC.
13. R. E. Urquhart, *Arnhem* (Los Angeles: Royal Publishing Company, 1958), p. 187.
14. Spaatz to Arnold, November 20, 1944, box 164, Spaatz Papers, LOC.
15. Eisenhower to Montgomery, September 20, 1944, *Papers*, p. 2164.
16. Montgomery to Eisenhower, September 21, 1944, *Eisenhower Papers*, p. 2165.
17. Montgomery to Bedell-Smith, September 21, 1944, *Eisenhower Papers*, p. 2175.
18. Eisenhower to Montgomery, October 9, 1944, *Papers*, p. 2215.
19. D. K. R. Crosswell, *Chief of Staff* (New York: Greenwood Press, 1991), p. 262.
20. *Ibid.*, p. 263.
21. Eisenhower to Montgomery, October 13, 1944, *Papers*, p. 2222.
22. *Ibid.*, p. 2225.
23. Harris to Tedder, November 1, 1944, AEAF Historical Record, AIR/1436, United Kingdom Public Record Office.

Chapter 12

1. Eisenhower to Marshall, August 18, 1944, *Papers*, p. 2073.
2. Blumenson, *Breakout and Pursuit*, pp. 565–568.
3. Hugh M. Cole, *The U.S. Army in World War II: The Lorraine Campaign* (Washington, D.C.: Center of Military History, 1950), p. 118.
4. Blumenson, *Breakout and Pursuit*, p. 669.
5. Historical records of the 10th Photographic Reconnaissance Group, USAFHRA.
6. Tom Ivie, *Aerial Reconnaissance* (Fallbrook, Calif.: Aero Publishers, 1981), p. 71.
7. Summary of XIX TAC's September operations, 537.4501, USAFHRA.
8. Historical records of the 405 Fighter Group, USAFHRA.
9. Historical records of the 362 Fighter Group, USAFHRA.
10. Craven and Cate, *Europe: ARGUMENT*, p. 266.
11. Summary of XIX TAC's September operations.
12. Cole, *Lorraine Campaign*, p. 53.
13. Gavin, *On to Berlin*, p. 140.
14. Patton, diary, September 8, 1944, *Papers*, p. 529.

15. *Ibid.*, p. 545.
16. Charles B. MacDonald and Sidney T. Matthews, "River Crossing at Arnaville," *Three Battles* (Washington, D.C.: Center of Military History, 1993), p.255.
17. *Ibid.*, p. 83.
18. *Ibid.*, p. 38.
19. Judith L. Bellaire, ed., *U.S. Army in World War II* (Washington, D.C.: Center of Military History, 1998), p. 255.
20. Lewis Sorley, *Thunderbolt* (New York: Simon & Schuster, 1992), p. 57.
21. Summary of XIX TAC's September operations.
22. *Ibid.*
23. Richard M. Ogorkiewicz, *Armor: A History of Mechanized Forces* (New York: Praeger, 1960), pp. 196–199.
24. Belton Y. Cooper, *Death Traps* (Novato, Calif.: Presidio Press, 1998), p. 91.
25. Sorley, *Thunderbolt*, p. 112.
26. Cole, *Lorraine Campaign*, p. 126.
27. Bradley, *Soldier's Story*, p. 427.
28. Cole, *Lorraine Campaign*, p. 154.
29. *Ibid.*, p. 177.
30. Historical records of the 406 Fighter Group, USAFHRA.
31. Historical records of the 405 Fighter Group, USAFHRA.
32. Patton, *Papers*, p. 559.
33. Third Army after-action reports, September 1944, 537.4501, USAFHRA.
34. Patton, *War as I Knew It*, pp. 119–120.
35. Historical records of the 405 Fighter Group.
36. Speidel, *Invasion 1944*, p. 147.

Chapter 13

1. Robert M. Lee, "History of IX Engineer Command," Lee Collection, 168.607-41, USAFHRA.
2. "A Report on the Combat Operations of XIX TAC," 537.04B, USAFHRA.
3. Historical records of the 362 Fighter Group.
4. Historical records of the 405 Fighter Group.
5. Historical records of the 406 Fighter Group, USAFHRA.
6. Historical records of the 435 Troop Carrier Group, USAFHRA.
7. Basil Collier, *Battle of the V-Weapons, 1944–1945* (New York: William Morrow, 1965), p. 148.
8. XIX TAC operations reports, October-November 1944, 537.02, USAFHRA.
9. Gail Wright, *832 Aviation Engineers Battalion History* (privately printed by the 832 Engineers Battalion, 1945), pp. 38–39.
10. David T. Griggs to Edward L. Bowles, February 22, 1945, 519.161-7, USAFHRA.
11. XIX TAC report, "Tactical Air Operations in the European Theater of Operations," 537.04A, USAFHRA.

12. Anthony Kemp, *Unknown Battle: Metz 1944* (New York: Stein and Day, 1981), p. 99.
13. Cole, *Lorraine Campaign*, pp. 272–273.
14. John Colby, *War from the Ground Up* (Austin, Tex.: Nortex Press, 1991), pp. 267–268.
15. XX Corps Artillery report, October 27, 1944, 533.4501-10, USAFHRA.
16. Patton, *Papers*, p. 537.
17. Spaatz, diary, October 22, 1944, box 3, Spaatz Papers, LOC.
18. Cole, *Lorraine Campaign*, p. 297.
19. T. Dodson Stamps and Vincent J. Esposito, eds., *Military History of World War II: Operations in the European Theater* (West Point, N.Y.: United States Military Academy, 1953), p. 461.

Chapter 14

1. Cole, *Lorraine Campaign*, p. 303.
2. Craven and Cate, *Europe: ARGUMENT*, p. 626.
3. Third Army after-action reports, November 1944, 537.4501, USAFHRA.
4. Cole, *Lorraine Campaign*, pp. 306–307.
5. *Ibid.*, pp. 321–325.
6. *Ibid.*, pp. 345–346.
7. *Ibid.*, p. 354.
8. *Ibid.*, pp. 471–480.
9. *Ibid.*, p. 373.
10. *Ibid.*, p. 416.
11. *Ibid.*, pp. 377–379.
12. *Ibid.*, p. 442.
13. *Ibid.*, pp. 407–408.
14. *Ibid.*, p. 517.
15. Third Army after-action reports, November 1944.
16. XIX TAC report, "Tactical Air Operations in Europe," 537.04A, USAFHRA.

Chapter 15

1. Craven and Cate, *Europe: ARGUMENT*, p. 679.
2. *Ibid.*, p. 682.
3. *Ibid.*, p. 686.
4. Hugh M. Cole, *The Ardennes: Battle of the Bulge* (Washington, D.C.: Office of the Chief of Military History, 1965), p. 422.
5. *Ibid.*, p. 510.
6. *Ibid.*, p. 526.
7. *Ibid.*, pp. 552–555.
8. Patton, *Papers*, p. 599.

9. Craven and Cate, *Europe: ARGUMENT*, pp. 682–701.
10. XIX TAC report, "Tactical Air Operations in Europe,"
11. Eisenhower, *Crusade in Europe*, pp. 377–378.
12. Bradley, *Soldier's Story*, p. 487.
13. Eisenhower, *Crusade in Europe*, p. 378.
14. Winston S. Churchill, *The Second World War: Triumph and Tragedy* (Boston: Houghton Mifflin Company, 1953), pp. 277–282.

Chapter 16

1. XIX TAC report, "Tactical Air Operations in Europe," 537.04A, USAFHRA.
2. Craven and Cate, *Europe: ARGUMENT*, pp. 557–562.
3. XXIX TAC ORS report no. 70., February 1, 1945, 533.3101, USAFHRA.
4. IX TAC ORS report no. 67, November 28, 1944, 533.310, USAFHRA.
5. Bradley to Spaatz, May 17, 1945, 138.4–36A, USAFHRA.
6. Report of General Omar N. Bradley and the Air Effect Committee, 12th Army Group, "Effect of Air Power on Military Operations: Western Europe," Special Collection, Air University Library, Maxwell AFB, Alabama.
7. Patton to Marshall, August 17, 1944, *Papers*, p. 517.
8. Patton to Arnold, August 17, 1944, *Papers*, p. 516.
9. *Ibid.*, p. 611.
10. Weyland oral history transcript, K239.0512–813, USAFHRA.
11. Stamps and Esposito, Eds., *Military History of World War II*, p. 440.

Bibliography

Arnold, Henry H. *Global Mission*. New York: Harper, 1949.
Aron, Robert. *France Reborn*. New York: Charles Scribner's Sons, 1964.
Baldwin, Hanson. *Tiger Jack*. Ft. Collins, Colorado: Old Army Press, 1979.
Baynes, John. *Urquhart of Arnhem*. New York: Brassey, 1993.
Beck, Alfred M., Abe Bortz, Charles W. Lynch, Lido Mayo, and Ralph F. Weld. *U.S. Army in World War II: Corps of Engineers: The War Against Germany*. Washington, D.C.: Center of Military History, 1985.
Bellaire, Judith L., ed. *U.S. Army in World War II*. Washington, D.C.: Center of Military History, 1998.
Bennett, Ralph. *Ultra in the West*. New York: Charles Scribner's Sons, 1979.
Blumenson, Martin. *Battle of the Generals*. New York: Morrow, 1993.
____. *Duel for France*. Boston: Houghton Mifflin, 1963.
____. *The U.S. Army in World War II: Breakout and Pursuit*. Washington, D.C.: Center of Military History, 1961.
Bradley, Omar N. *A Soldier's Story*. New York: Henry Holt, 1951.
Brereton, Lewis H. *Brereton Diaries*. New York: William Morrow, 1946.
Bryant, Arthur. *Triumph in the West*. Garden City, N.Y.: Doubleday and Company, Inc., 1959.
Bykofsky, Joseph, and Harold Larson. *U.S. Army in World War II: The Transportation Corps: Operations Overseas*. Washington, D.C.: Office of the Chief of Military History, 1957.
Cary, James. *Tanks and Armor in Modern Warfare*. New York: Franklin Watts, Inc., 1966.
Churchill, Winston S. *The Second World War: Triumph and Tragedy*. Boston: Houghton Mifflin Company, 1953.
Claydon, Anthony. *Three Marshals of France*. New York: Brassey, 1992.
Colby, John. *War from the Ground Up*. Austin, Texas: Nortex Press, 1996.
Cole, Hugh M. *The U.S. Army in World War II: The Ardennes: The Battle of the Bulge*. Washington, D.C.: Office of the Chief of Military History, 1965
____. *The U.S. Army in World War II: The Lorraine Campaign*. Washington, D.C.: Historical Division, U.S. Army, 1950.

Collier, Basil. *Battle of the V-Weapons, 1944–1945.* New York: William Morrow, 1965.
Cooling, Benjamin F., ed. *Case Studies in the Development of Close Air Support.* Washington, D.C.: Office of Air Force History, 1990.
Cooper, Belton Y. *Death Traps.* Novato, California: Presidio Press, 1998.
Cowburn, Benjamin. *No Cloak, No Dagger.* London: Jarolds Publisher Ltd., 1960.
Craven, W.F., and J.L. Cate, eds. *The Army Air Forces in World War II.* Chicago: University of Chicago Press, 1951.
_____ and _____. *Europe: ARGUMENT to V-E Day, January 1944 to May 1945.* Chicago: University of Chicago Press, 1951.
_____ and _____. *Men and Planes.* Chicago: University of Chicago Press, 1951.
Crosswell, D.K.R. *Chief of Staff.* New York: Greenwood Press, 1991.
De Guingand, Francis. *Generals at War.* London: Hodder and Stoughton, 1964.
D'Este, Carlo. *Decision in Normandy.* New York: E. P. Dutton, Inc., 1983.
_____. *Patton: A Genius for War.* New York: Harper Collins, 1995.
Donahue, William, T. Cunningham, and H. Pattison. *Clarke of St. Vith.* Cleveland: Dillon, Liederbach, 1974.
Dreux, William B. *No Bridges Blown.* Notre Dame: University of Notre Dame Press, 1971.
Dunn, William R. *Fighter Pilot.* Lexington, Kentucky: University of Kentucky Press, 1982.
Eisenhower, Dwight D. *Crusade in Europe.* Garden City, N.Y.: Doubleday, 1948.
_____. *The Papers of Dwight David Eisenhower.* Alfred D. Chandler, ed. Baltimore: The Johns Hopkins University Press, 1970.
Foot, M.R.D. *SOE in France.* London: HMSO, 1966.
Fourth Armored Division Association. *Legacy of the 4th Armored Division.* Paducah, Kentucky: Turner Publishing Company, 1990.
Gavin, James M. *On to Berlin.* New York: Viking Press, 1978.
Golley, John. *The Day of the Typhoon.* Wellingborough, U.K.: Patrick Stephens, 1986.
Hallion, Richard P. *D-Day 1944.* Washington, D.C.: Air Force History and Museums Program, 1994.
Hinsley, F.H., et al. *British Intelligence in the Second World War.* New York: Cambridge University Press, 1988.
Holt, Harold Norman. "Column Cover." *Journal of the American Aviation Historical Society.* Spring, 1984.
Horrocks, Brian. *Escape to Action.* New York: St. Martin's Press, 1960.
Infield, Glenn B. *Unarmed and Unafraid.* New York: Macmillan, 1970.
Ivie, Tom. *Aerial Reconnaissance.* Fallbrook, California: Aero Publishers, Inc., 1981.
Kemp, Anthony. *Unknown Battle: Metz, 1944.* New York: Stein and Day, 1981.

Kozaczuk, Wladyslaw. *Enigma*. Frederick, Maryland: University Publications of America, Inc., 1984.
Kreis, John F. *Piercing the Fog*. Washington, D.C.: Air Force History and Museums Program, 1996.
Lamb, Richard. *Montgomery in Europe, 1943–45*. New York: Franklin Watts, 1984.
Liddell-Hart, B.H. *History of the Second World War*. London: Cassell & Company, 1970.
Lucas, James, and James Barker. *Battle of Normandy*. New York: Holmes & Meier, Inc., 1978.
MacDonald, Charles B. *Command Decisions*. Washington, D.C.: Center of Military History, 1990.
Maule, Henry. *Out of the Sand*. London: Oldhams Books Ltd., 1966.
Messinger, Charles. *Bomber Harris*. New York: St. Martin's Press, 1984.
Middlebrook, Martin. *Arnhem 1944*. San Francisco: Westview Press, 1994.
Montgomery, Bernard. *Normandy to the Baltic*. London: Hutchinson & Company, Ltd., 1948.
Murray, Williamson. *Strategy for Defeat*. Maxwell Air Force Base, Alabama: Air University Press, 1983.
Ogorkiewicz, Richard M. *Armor: A History of Mechanized Forces*. New York: Frederick A. Praeger, 1960.
Ohl, John K. *Supplying the Troops*. De Kalb, Illinois: Northern Illinois University Press, 1994.
Patton, George S., Jr. *The Patton Papers*. Martin Blumenson, ed. Boston: Houghton Mifflin Company, 1974.
_____. *War as I Knew It*. Boston: Houghton Mifflin Company 1947.
Pogue, Forrest C. *The Supreme Command*. Washington, D.C.: Office of the Chief of Military History, 1954.
Price, Frank J. *Troy H. Middleton*. Baton Rouge, Louisiana: Louisiana State University Press, 1974.
Reit, Seymour. *Masquerade*. New York: Hawthorne Books, Inc., 1978.
Ruppenthal, Roland G. *Logistical Support of the Armies, September 1944 — May 1945*. Washington, D.C.: Center of Military History, 1995.
_____. "Logistics and the Broad-Front Strategy." *Command Decisions*. Washington, D.C.: Center of Military History, 1990.
Shulman, Milton. *Defeat in the West*. London: Secker and Warburg, 1947.
Smith, Walter Bedell. *Eisenhower's Six Great Decisions*. New York: Longmans, Green and Company, 1956.
Sorley, Lewis. *Thunderbolt: General Creighton Abrams and the Army of His Times*. New York: Simon & Schuster, 1992.
Speidel, Hans. *Invasion 1944*. Chicago: Henry Regnery Company, 1950.
Stacey, C.P. *The Canadian Army, 1939–1945*. Ottowa: King's Printer, 1948.
Stamps, T. Dodson, and Vincent J. Esposito, eds. *Military History of World War*

II: Operations in the European Theater. West Point, N.Y.: United States Military Academy, 1953.

Strategic Services Unit, War Department. *War Report of the OSS*. New York: Walker & Company, 1976.

Thompson, G.R., and Dixie R. Harris. *The Signal Corps*. Washington, D.C.: Center of Military History, 1966.

Urquhart, R.E. *Arnhem*. Los Angeles: Royal Publishing Company, 1958.

U.S. Army 90th Infantry Division. *A History of the 90th Infantry Division in World War II*. Baton Rouge, Louisiana: Army and Navy Publishing Company, 1946.

Van Crevald, Martin. *Supplying War*. New York: Cambridge University Press, 1977.

Von Luck, Hans. *Panzer Commander*. New York: Praeger, 1989.

Warner, Philip. *Horrocks*. London: Hamish Hamilton, 1984.

Wolfe, Martin. *Green Light*. Washington, D.C.: Center for Air Force History, 1993.

Index

A-20 light bomber 30–31, 60, 62
Aachen 114
Abrams, Lt. Col. Creighton 122, 154
Air Corps Tactical school 36
Air Forces *see* specific units
Air liaison officers *see* Liaison personnel
Air supply *see* Supplies
Air supremacy 3, 14, 23–24, 34, 47, 102, 161
Airborne forces *see* First Allied Airborne Army and specific units
Aircraft equipment 44–47
Aircraft types *see* specific types
Airfields 63–67, 96, 106, 110, 136–137
Alençon 75, 79
Allied Expeditionary Air Forces 3, 36, 53–54, 78
Allison engine *see* P-51; P-38
Anderson, Brig. Gen. S. E. 12
Angers 56, 90
Anti-aircraft artillery 29, 49, 99, 121, 137–138
Anti-tank weapons 17, 141
Antwerp 103, 114–118, 120
Ardennes 149–156
Argentan 74–78
Argonne Forest 95
Armies *see* specific units
Armored Column Cover 12, 43, 72, 160
Armored divisions 15–16, 18; *see also* specific units
Army Air Forces 3, 5, 36, 41, 68, 103
Army Groups: 6th 134; 12th 15, 78, 88, 115, 118; 21st 6, 95
Arnaville 127
Arnhem 115–117
Arnold, Gen. H. H. 3, 110–111, 118, 162
Arracourt 129
Artillery 15, 17, 26, 40, 43, 53, 131, 135, 139, 143, 149
Assenois 154

Aviation engineers *see* Engineers
Avranches 15, 18, 19

B-24 109
B-26 29–31, 49, 60, 62, 69, 99, 111, 130, 150, 154
Barges 82
Bastogne 151–155
Bazooka 18
Black market 104
Blois 56
Bocage 9
Bomb fuses 77, 160
Bomb loads 29, 31, 44–49
Bomber Command (RAF) 3–4, 109
bombsights 49
Boulogne 26
Bradley, Gen. Omar: air support 160; Argentan 74–78, 84; Brest 24, 100; British 84; Chambois 79; Dempsey 84; FAAA 104; French 102; Gavin Gerow 79; interdiction 33, 161; Loire 126; MARKET-GARDEN 116; Metz 131; Montgomery 116, 149, 15; Mortain 53; Orléans 111; Patton 23; Paris 88; pause 81; Quesada 10, 44; St. Lô 14; St. Malo 26; Seine 77; supplies 101; 12th Army Gp 15; ULTRA 51
Brereton, Lt. Gen. Lewis 3, 4, 8, 37, 62, 106, 117
Brest 14, 24–26, 58, 96–100
Bridges 19, 69, 70, 86, 128, 135, 147, 154
Brittany 17–33, 96–100; *see also* Brest
Brussels 115
Bulge *see* Ardennes
Bulldozer 55, 103
Burnon 153

C-47 38–39, 54, 65–66, 89, 154
Caen 9, 14

Camouflage 38, 80
Carpet bombing 14, 38, 161
Casualties 76, 79, 84, 90, 93, 97, 110, 116, 127, 138, 139–149, 146, 147
Cavalry 15, 17, 24
CCA 92, 95, 109–110, 124, 129, 138, 154
CCB 146
Cézembre, Isle de 29
Châlons-sur-Marne 78, 95, 122, 136
Chambois 79
Chambrey 133
Charmes 132
Chartres 58, 65, 66, 71, 90, 126
Châteaudun 61, 65
Château-Salins 129, 145
Cherbourg 10, 142
Choltitz, Dietrich von 87–88
Churchill, Prime Minister Winston S. 155
Civilians 37, 65, 76
Clarke, Col. Bruce C. 21, 91, 152
COBRA 14
Collins, Maj. Gen. J. Lawton 10, 14
Combined Chiefs of Staff 5
Commands *see* specific units
Commercy 122
Communications 22, 25, 42, 51, 71, 73, 123
COM Z *see* Supplies
Conflans Ste. Honorine 83
Coningham, Air Chief Marshal 3, 4
Cook, Maj. Gen. Gilbert 7, 17, 91–92, 121
Corps: composition 17; Second Corps (Canadian) 79; III Corps 153–154; VII Corps 14; VIII Corps 17, 19, 32, 91–100, 152; XII Corps 17, 21–23, 91–95, 121, 123, 133, 145–147; XV Corps 17, 74–84, 121, 130–133, 151; XX Corps 17, 55–57, 90, 121–128, 143, 147–149; XXX Corps (UK) 116
Counterattack 53–54, 151–155
Couriers *see* Communications
Crerer, Gen. Henry D. 6, 8,
CROSSBOW 113

Darmstadt 130
De Gaulle, Gen. Charles 32, 80, 87–88
Dempsey, Lt. Gen. Miles 6, 84
Dieulbuard 128
Dieuze 141, 144, 146
Dinan 25–26
Dive bombing 46, 49
Dives River 79
Divisions: 1st Airborne (UK) 118; 82nd Airborne 80, 116–117, 152; 101st Airborne 116–117, 152, 154; 1st Armored (Polish) 79; 2nd Armored (Fr.) 75–79, 80, 88, 132; 2nd Panzer 79; 2nd SS Panzer 77; 4th Armored 20, 23, 91–94, 125, 128–129, 145–147, 153–154; 5th Armored 75–76, 82; 5th Infantry 90, 122–123, 127, 131, 147, 149; 6th Armored 24–26, 133, 145, 147; 7th Armored 122, 126, 132; 10th Armored 147, 149; 26th Infantry 145–147; 30th Infantry 53; 35th Infantry 90, 121, 128, 133, 145–146; 79th Infantry 74, 82–83, 133; 80th Infantry 79, 85, 90, 121, 126, 133, 128, 145–147; 83rd Infantry 27–30; 90th Infantry 74, 79, 121, 147–148; 95th Infantry 147–149
Doctrine 36
Dompaire 132
Doolittle, Maj. Gen. James 3, 8, 109
Dornot 127
Dreux 66, 126
Droptanks 44, 47, 134

Eberbach, Gen. Heinrich 51
Eddy, Maj. Gen. Manton S. 121, 123, 125, 131, 143, 145, 147
832nd Aviation Engineers Battalion *see* Engineers
Eighth Air Force 33, 36, 45, 49, 148, 154
Eisenhower, Gen. Dwight: AEAF 44; airlift 106, 109; Antwerp 101, 113–113; Ardennes 151–152, 155; Bradley 51, 155; Brest 100; Cook 121; de Gaulle 87, 102; directive 125; FAAA 107; Falaise 78, 80, 84; French 102; Gavin 80; Harris 5; injury 113; Leigh-Mallory 5; liaison airplane 68; Marshall 87, 113, 155; Montgomery 95, 113–116, 112, 120, 151; Paris 86, 88, 102; Patton 23, 100; ports 101; railroads 100–101 SHAEF 3, 113; supplies 100–101; ULTRA 52; West Point 3; Wood 21
Elbeuf 84–85
Engineers 17, 62–69, 96, 111, 112, 121, 127, 128, 147, 149
Enigma 52
Evacuation 61, 110, 138
Exploitation 21, 23, 162

F-5, F-6 airplanes 59–60
FAAA *see* First Allied Airborne Army
Falaise 74–81
FFI *see* Resistance
15th Air Force 5
15th Tactical Reconnaissance Squadron 125

Index

Fighter-bomber: airfields 63–66, 107; armored column cover 42, 43, 160; artillery 38, 140; bombs 44; Brest 98; COBRA 14; Dieuze dam 141–142; dive bombing 49; Falaise 80; Fôret de Gremecey 133; ground support 42–50, 135–137, 140; liaison airplanes 68; mobility 12; Mortain 553; OMAHA Beach 38; P-38 47; P-47 45; P-51 46; railroads 135; St. Malo 29; strafing 39, 40, 50; tactical reconnaissance 73
Fighter Groups: 36th 80; 354th 135; 358th 135, 137; 362nd 82, 100, 124, 136, 140, 141; 363rd 80; 373rd 56; 405th 125, 130, 135, 137; 406th 85, 98, 124, 133, 137; 467th 107
First Allied Airborne Army 34, 106–107, 113, 115–117
First Army 6, 8, 84, 101, 132, 148
First Canadian Army 74, 77–79
Fountainebleau 90, 122
438th Troop Carrier Group 109, 122, 145
435 Troop Carrier Group 137
14th Liaison Squadron 68
Frankfurt 125, 130
Fronts 122, 145

Gaffey, Maj. Gen. Hugh 79, 153
Gasoline 18, 22, 45, 47, 80, 92, 95–96, 104, 106, 108, 110, 123
Gavin, Maj. Gen. James 80, 117
German Air Force 36, 38, 161
Gerow, Maj. Gen. Leonard T. 79, 108, 110, 123, 125, 134
Gestapo 53
Glide bombing 49
Gliders 117
Granville 27, 113
Ground Liaison Officer *see* Liaison personnel
Ground support 10, 12, 14, 36, 34–50
Grow, Maj. Gen. Robert 24–26, 98

Haislip, Maj. Gen. Wade 7, 74–76, 81, 82, 88, 89
Harris, Air Chief Marshal Arthur 5–6, 71, 120
Headquarters 62, 136, 72–73
Helfers, Maj. M. C. 52
Hitler, Adolf 26, 51, 52, 120, 123, 125, 143, 144

Intelligence 38, 42, 51, 58–60, 91, 98, 112; *see also* Reconnaissance

Interdiction 14, 32, 36, 37, 50, 55–56, 59, 69–71, 124, 157, 160

Jerricans 22, 107–108
Joinville 122

Kluge, Field Marshal Gunther von 23, 40, 51–52, 74
Koenigsmacher 148

L-4, L-5 airplanes *see* Liaison aircraft
Leaflets 124
Leclerc, Gen. Jacques 74–76, 80–81, 87–88
Lee, Lt. Gen. John C. 100–102
Le Havre 26, 84, 114
Leigh-Mallory Air Chief Marshal 3, 5, 6, 53, 71
Le Mans 65–66, 69
Liaison aircraft 21, 24, 38, 61, 67–68, 113, 128
Liaison personnel 42, 73, 98, 160
Light bomber *see* A-20 light bomber
Loing River 61
Loire River 36, 55, 127, 132
Lorient 23, 100
Luck, Hans von 84
Lunéville 133
Luxembourg 152

Machine guns 45–48
Macon, Maj. Gen. Robert 29
Mainz 143
Maisons-Lafitte 83, 85
Maizieres-les-Metz 140
Mantes-Gassicourt 82–83, 86
MARKET-GARDEN 116–118
Marne River 95, 122
Marne-Rhine Canal 144
Marshall, Gen. George 87, 107, 113, 155
Medical 18, 110, 138, 140, 150
Mediterranean Theater 5, 134
Medium bomber *see* B-26
Melun 126
Metz 114, 124, 128, 131–132, 135, 139–140, 143, 148–149
Meuse River 95, 122–123, 134, 150, 152, 154
Middleton, Maj. Gen. Troy 17, 19, 22, 97, 100
Military police 15, 18
Milly 90
Mines 66, 145–146
Mittersheim 147
Montgomery, Field Marshal Bernard: Ardennes 151, 155; Argentan 84; Bradley

78, 88, 155; command 6, 8, 89; Crerar 6, 79; Eisenhower 3, 8, 9, 113–115, 118–120, 155; FAAA 113; Falaise 74, 80; MARKET-GARDEN 112–120; offensive 113–119; Paris 88; Patton 134; supplies 116; Tedder 5; ULTRA 52; Vernon 119
Morhange 145–146
Mortain 51–54, 74
Moselle River 95, 122–132
Mustang *see* P-51

Nancy 128–129, 132–133
Nantes 23, 56, 100
Napalm 12, 26, 29, 50
Netherlands 115–117
Neufchâteau 153
Night operations 37, 38, 60, 135
XIX Tactical Air Command: airfields, 54, 62–64, 136; anti-aircraft fire 142, 144; Ardennes 154; August record 74, 88; bomb load 44, 64; Brest 98; commendations 162, 89; communications 71–73, 154; Delme 144; Dieuze 140–142; enlarged 54; Elster 125; Falaise 79; fighter groups 34, 129, 151–152; Fôret de Grémecey 133; Fort Driant 138–139; headquarters 73; Metz 139; Moselle 133; moves 62; night operations 137; Ninth AF 10; November operations 143–146; Paris 84; priorities 124–125; reconnaissance 60, 133; September record 124–128; sorties 41; tactical radius 44
Ninth Air Force 5, 8, 10, 13, 36, 41, 42, 45, 59, 60, 73, 97–98, 135, 151
IX Air Force Service Command 12, 105, 141
Ninth Army 58
IX Bomber Command 12, 29, 71, 129
IX Engineer Command 62–67
IX Tactical Air Command 10–12, 37, 151
IX Troop Carrier Command 12, 106–109, 117–118, 154
Nogent-sur-Seine 122
Normandy 9, 36, 38, 66, 70, 81, 85, 92

Oil campaign 36, 85
OMAHA Beach 38
Operational Research Section 30, 31, 99, 154, 159
Ordnance 17, 142, 154
Orléans 58, 91–92
OVERLORD 3, 6, 10, 62, 102, 109

P-38 26, 29, 34, 47–50
P-47 34, 44–46, 62, 82, 128, 141

P-51 34, 44–47, 59, 61–62, 125
Panzer divisions 9, 38–39, 51, 53, 73, 79, 81, 84–85, 88, 92, 116, 132–133, 151
Panzerfaust 93
Paris 66, 80–81, 86–89, 102, 135
Pas-de-Calais 15, 113
Patton, Lt. Gen. George: Ardennes 150–155; Argentan 74–79, 82; Avranches 17; biography 7; Bradley 77, 126, 131; Brest 17, 24–26, 96–100; Chambois 79; command maxims 18, 21, 72; commendations 89, 162; deception operations 15; engineers 69; Falaise 74–79, 81; flanks 54, 71, 132; Fôret de Grémecey 133; French 32; Gavin 80, 87; German offensives 51, 150–155; Grow 24–26; headquarters 73; interdiction 33; Leclerc 80; liaison airplanes 58, 68; Metz 131; Montgomery 134, 151; Moselle 120, 125, 129; XIX TAC 36, 89, 162; 90th Division 148; November offensive 143–150; operation pauses 95, 134, 143; Quiberon 19; railroad 69; reconnaissance 44; St. Malo 27; Seine 82; 7th Armored Division 126; supplies 79, 95, 101–102, 103, 109, 134; TUSA 17; ULTRA 52; Weyland 36, 44, 162
Perforated steel plank 65–67
Photographic reconnaissance *see* Reconnaissance
Polish forces 77, 79, 85
Polish mathematicians 52
Pont-à-Mousson 126, 143
Pontaubault 19, 24
Pontoise 89
Portal, Air Marshal Charles 6
Ports 15, 26, 70, 98, 101, 112, 115, 134
Pournoy-la-Chétive 132
Prefabricated Hessian Surfacing 63–64

Quesada, Maj. Gen. Elwood 6, 10–12, 37, 44
Quiberon 19, 22

Radar 9, 50, 137–138
Radio *see* Communications
Railroads 50, 67, 69–70, 71, 100–102, 104, 112, 124, 130, 135–137, 154
Reconnaissance 15, 33, 38, 44, 48–49, 55, 68–69, 73, 125
Red Ball Express *see* Trucks
Reims 67, 71, 91, 122, 125
Remonville 154
Rennes 19–22, 61, 65

Index

Resistance 1–33, 51, 54, 71, 87, 122–124, 133
Rhine River 114, 115, 116 118, 126, 134, 152
Rockets 12, 46, 53, 80, 136
Rommel, Field Marshal Erwin 40
Roosevelt, Pres. Franklin D. 156
Rouen 83–85
Royal Air Force 3, 5, 138
Ruhr 114–115, 125
Rundstedt, Field Marshal Gerd von 125, 145

Saar 113–115, 125, 136, 149
Saarbrucken 143
Saarlautern 149
Sabotage 71
St. Dizier 66, 67, 136–137
St. Germain-en-Lay 83, 85
St. Hilaire-du-Harcouet 69
St. Lô 14
St. Malo 26–30
St. Mihiel 123
St. Nazaire 26
St. Vith 152
Ste. Geneviève 128
Sarre River 126, 145, 147, 149
Schelde 115, 120, 125
Second Army (UK) 84
Second Engineer Brigade 67
Second Tactical Air Force (RAF) 3, 54, 80
Seille River 145–146
Seine River 15, 54, 69, 81–89
Sherman tank *see* Tanks
Shipping 118
Siegfried Line 114, 124, 125, 134, 147
Signals *see* Communications
Sillegny 132
Silvester, Maj. Gen. Lindsay 126
Smith, Lt. Gen. Walter 118
Sorties 48, 80, 88, 137
Spaatz, Lt. Gen., Carl 3, 9, 85, 118, 141
Square Mesh Track 69
Strafing *see* Interdiction
Strategic bombing 36, 161
Supercharger 45
Supplies: air supply 65–67, 109–112, 140, 154; air supremacy 36; airfields 65–67; armored divisions 18; beaches 101; Bradley 101–103; Brest 23–26, 98–100; Chartres 66; COM Z 86, 100–104, 96, 144; engineers 65–67; heavy bombers 66; interdiction 36; liaison airplanes 67; logistics 102; morale 143; Paris 86–88, 102; Patton 102; Ports 96–100, 134, 142; railroads 104; Red Ball Express 103–104; 6th Armored Division 25; trucks 103–104; winter clothing 137

Tactical radius 44–46
Tank destroyers 123, 129
Tanks 18, 21, 38, 79–81, 92–93, 129–133, 143, 146
Tedder, Air Chief Marshal Arthur 3, 5, 39, 109
Telegraph 71
Telephone 71
10th Photographic Reconnaissance Group 60
Thionville 126, 131, 139
Third U.S. Army: air reconnaissance 58, 61; Ardennes 150–154; Avranches 15, 18; commendations 162; communications 72–73; corps 17; cut-off risk 51; defensive 133; Dieuze 141; flanks 54, 58, 132; 14th Liaison Squadron 66; headquarters 72; Le Mans 65; Metz 131; Montgomery 114; officers 7, 57; Operational pauses 124; OVERLORD 8; Seine 54, 85; supplies 101–102, 113; tactics 19; training 140
31st Photographic Reconnaissance Squadron 124
37th Tank Battalion 154
Track cuts *see* Interdiction
Transport aircraft *see* C-47
Trucks 95, 102–104, 123–124, 141, 154
XXIX TAC 56, 151
Twining, Maj. Gen. Nathan 5
Typhoon aircraft (RAF) 53, 80

Uckange 144, 148
ULTRA *see* Intelligence
U.S. Strategic Air Forces 3

Vandenberg, Maj. Gen. Hoyt 12–13, 34, 36, 98, 129, 137, 147
Vannes 19
Vaucouleurs 122
Verdun 122, 123, 126, 136
Vernon 83, 119, 122
Versailles 69
Vitry-le-François 122
V-Weapons 113, 115, 137–138

Walker, Maj. Gen. Walton 55–57, 126, 132, 140
War Department (U.S.) 103, 138

Weather 37, 63, 110–111, 129, 134, 135, 140–141, 154
West Wall *see* Siegfried Line
Weyland, Maj. Gen. Otto: artillery 43; biography 34–35; commendations 89, 162; Elster 125; Fôret de Grémecey 133; interdiction 34–36; Loire 56; XIX TAC command 12; Patton 36, priorities 36; officers 57
Wood, Maj. Gen. John 20–21, 23, 91–92